Staffordshire Figures

1780–1840

Equestrians, Entertainers, Personalities, Biblical Figures, & Sportsmen

Volume 2

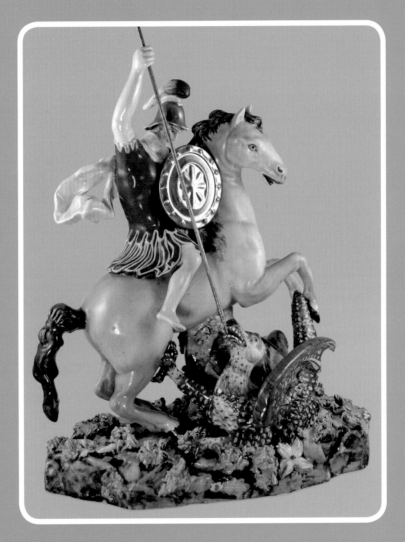

Myrna Schkolne

4880 Lower Valley Road • Atglen, PA 19310

Dedication

Dedicated to the memory of Staffordshire's potters,
without whom none of this would have happened.

Other Schiffer Books by the Author:
*Staffordshire Figures 1780 to 1840 Volume 1: Manufacturers, Pastimes, &
Work.* ISBN: 978-0-7643-4537-1. $69.99

Other Schiffer Books on Related Subjects:
Staffordshire Figures: History in Earthenware 1740-1900. Adele Kenny
& Veronica Moriarty. ISBN: 978-0-7643-1917-4. $59.95
*Victorian Staffordshire Figures 1835-1875, Book One: Portraits, Navy &
Military, Theatrical & Literary Characters.* A. & N. Harding. ISBN:
978-0-7643-0464-4. $95.00

Copyright © 2014 by Myrna Schkolne

Library of Congress Control Number: 2013944801

Cover designed by Bruce Waters
Type set in Garamond UltraCondensed/Arrus BT

ISBN: 978-0-7643-4538-8
Printed in China

Published by Schiffer Publishing, Ltd.
4880 Lower Valley Road
Atglen, PA 19310
Phone: (610) 593-1777; Fax: (610) 593-2002
E-mail: Info@schifferbooks.com

For our complete selection of fine books on this and related subjects,
please visit our website at www.schifferbooks.com. You may also
write for a free catalog.

This book may be purchased from the publisher. Please try your
bookstore first.

We are always looking for people to write books on new and
related subjects. If you have an idea for a book, please contact us
at proposals@schifferbooks.com

Schiffer Publishing's titles are available at special discounts for bulk
purchases for sales promotions or premiums. Special editions,
including personalized covers, corporate imprints, and excerpts can
be created in large quantities for special needs. For more information,
contact the publisher.

Volume 2
Contents

About Values and Titles

Values

This work uses the following scale as an approximation of value.

Price A: Up to $1,000 (£625)
Price B: $1,001–$3,000 (£626–£1,875)
Price C: $3,001–$6,000 (£1,876–£3,750)
Price D: $6,001–$9,000 (£3,751–£5,626)
Price E: $9,001–$15,000 (£5,626–£9,375)
Price F: $15,001–$25,000 (£9,376–£15,625
Price G: $25,001 & over (£15,626 & above)

The value of a figure is a function of the standard of its modeling and decoration, its condition, its scarcity, and the appeal of the subject. Essentially, value is quirky, and it can be somewhat subjective. Many small figures are highly desirable and difficult to procure, yet they fall into Price A—even though collectors value them more highly than mediocre figures in higher price brackets.

The determinants of value are not apparent from a photograph, and seemingly identical figures may have vastly different values. The values indicated in captions are not auction values or resale values. Rather, they are the values of figures purchased from a reputable retail source. In each case, the value is an estimate of the value of the figure illustrated. A very similar figure may be worth significantly more or less, depending on the condition and the quality of the glazes and enamels. At the same time, condition issues are not always apparent in a photograph, and, out of respect for those supplying photographs of their treasures for this work, condition reports have not been attached to captions. For that reason, condition is only factored into the value equation to the extent that issues are apparent in the photograph or are known to the author.

Titles

Please note that figure titles are frequently misspelled and have been reproduced in the captions as they appear on the figures.

31. Equestrians

The equestrian figures shown here depict the colorfully attired ladies and gentlemen who were the circus stars of their day. In the late eighteenth century, Philip Astley transformed the embryonic entertainment of trick riding into the entertainment genre known as the circus. That circus was very different from today's circus, and equestrian acts dominated. Routines evolved to include clowns, acrobats, learned animals, performing monkeys and dogs, and the occasional exhibition of an exotic animal, but for decades the circus was about equestrianism. Hippodrama became a distinct entertainment, and the circus staged spectacular reenactments of military battles and hunts, the latter even including foxes and dogs.

Women equestriennes featured prominently in the early circus, and female figures show women in their starring roles. Circus reenactments allowed women to participate avidly in sports denied beyond the circus, and, for this reason, earthenware equestriennes are portrayed in hunting roles. Some equestrian figures portray military gentlemen. It is tempting to try to identify these dashing gentlemen as one or other of the military heroes of the past, but, in reality, many military portraits were painted with the riders posed just as they are for earthenware figures. Rare female figures pair with some of these male military figures, supporting the conviction that the figures represent circus stars of their day.

Equestrian figures of King William III, Hudibras, and Dick Turpin are shown elsewhere in this work.

Figure 31.2. Lady on horseback. Attributed to Patriotic Group. H: 9.1". The horse is painted to resemble a zebra to mimic a circus routine of the day. The distinctive base supports the attribution. Price E. *Brighton and Hove Museums.*

Figure 31.1. Lady and gentleman on horseback, with spill vase. Attributed to Leather Leaf Group. H: 8.1". Both flower forms on the base are characteristic of the Group, as is the distinctive painting style. Price E. *Brighton and Hove Museums.*

Figure 31.3. Gentleman and lady on horseback, a pair. Attributed to Patriotic Group. H: 9.4" (L), 9.5" (R). Price F.

Figure 31.4. Gentleman and lady on horseback, a pair. Attributed to Patriotic Group. H: 9.3". Like the previous pair, but the tops of the bases are painted in a colorful pattern. There are tiny spurs behind his shoes. Price F.

Figure 31.5. Gentleman and lady on horseback, detail of the previous pair.

Figure 31.6. Gentleman on horseback. Probably attributable to Patriotic Group. H: 9.3". The base is only otherwise recorded on figures attributable to the Patriotic Group, but the painting is atypical. Price C. *The William Herbert and Nancy Hunt Collection.*

Figure 31.7. Lady on horseback. H: ~9.1". The horse, like figure 31.2, is painted to mimic a zebra, and the dress pattern is in the Patriotic Group manner, but the figure exhibits no other Patriotic Group characteristics. Price E. *The Moore Collection.*

Figure 31.8. Gentleman and lady on horseback, an assembled pair. H: 9.5". Note the painting atop her base and the luster decoration on his base. Price E. *Photograph Courtesy of Sotheby's, Inc. © 2014.*

Figure 31.9. Gentleman and lady on horseback, a pair. H: ~9.5". From the same figure molds as Patriotic Group examples, but the painting style differs and the modeling is not as crisp. Price E. *John Howard; www. antiquepottery.co.uk.*

Figure 31.11. Gentleman on horseback, with a dog, with bocage. Attributed to Leather Leaf Group. H: ~9.5". Bocage is very uncommon with such large equestrians, as is the dog. Same base as previous examples. A similar pair (gentleman and lady) is recorded, both having dogs and Leather Leaf Group bocages. Price E.

Figure 31.10. Gentleman on horseback. H: 9.5". From the same figure molds as Patriotic Group examples but lacks features to support attribution. Price D. *James D. Julia Auctioneers, Fairfield, Maine; www.jamesdjulia.com.*

Figure 31.12. Gentleman and lady on horseback, a pair. H: ~8.5". The unusual bases are known only from this pair. Price F. *Photograph Courtesy of Sotheby's, Inc.* © 2014.

Figure 31.13. Military officer on horseback. H: ~10". Price D. *John Howard; www.antiquepottery.co.uk.*

Figure 31.14. Military officer on horseback. H: ~10". Unlike the previous figure in that the officer now has a sword at his side and the support beneath the horse is different. Price D. *John Howard; www.antiquepottery.co.uk.*

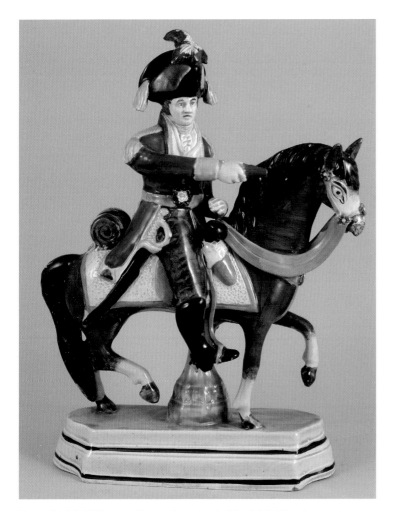

Figure 31.15. Military officer on horseback. H: 10.2". Like the previous figure, but differences in painting impart great individuality. Price D. *Andrew Dando Antiques.*

Figure 31.16. Military officer on horseback. H: 9.8". Quite different from previous examples and rarer. This model pairs with the following equestrienne. Price E. *Bonhams.*

Figure 31.17. Lady on horseback. H: 9". Probably pairs with the previous equestrian as both horses have raised front legs. Known from only this example. Price E. © *Fitzwilliam Museum, Cambridge.*

Figure 31.18. Gentleman and lady on horseback, he with a dog, a pair, with bocages. H: 6.7". Equestrian figures with bocages are generally on a smaller scale than those without, and the gentleman frequently has a dog. Probably from the same pot bank as the following four figures. Price E. *Andrew Dando Antiques.*

Figure 31.19. Lady on horseback, with bocage. H: 6". Similar to the previous equestrienne but with different bocage leaves and with the flowers arranged in clusters. Price B.

Figure 31.20. Gentleman on horseback, with a dog, with bocage. H: 6.3". Like the small male equestrian in figure 31.18, but here the bocage flowers are in clusters of threes. Price C.

Figure 31.21. Gentleman on horseback, with a dog, with bocage. H: ~6.3". The bocage flowers are as on the previous figure, but here the bocage has cilantro leaves rather than fern leaves. Both figures are probably from the same pot bank. Price C.

Figure 31.22. Gentleman on horseback, with bocage. H: ~6.3". The horse is striped like a zebra because this figure mimics a circus routine. The unusual bocage leaves are unpainted on the reverse. Possibly from the same pot bank as the previous four examples. Price C.

Figure 31.23. Gentleman on horseback, with a dog, with bocage. Probably attributable to Leather Leaf Group. H: ~7.5". The flowers are not specific to the Group, but the bocage leaves and the base support attribution. A companion equestrienne is recorded. Price C. *The Moore Collection.*

Figure 31.24. Gentleman on horseback, with a dog, with bocage. Attributed to Hall. H: 6.9". These six-petalled bocage flowers are specific to Hall. Price C. *The Bowes Museum, Barnard Castle.*

Figure 31.25. Lady on horseback, with a dog, with bocage. Attributed to Hall. H: ~6.9". Pairs with the previous figure and has the same bocage flowers. Price C. *The Moore Collection.*

Figure 31.26. Lady on horseback, with a dog, but with bocage. Attributed to Hall. H: ~6.9". Like the previous figure with different bocage flowers. These star-shaped bocage flowers are specific to Hall. Their colors and large yellow centers are typical of Hall flowers. Price C.

Figure 31.27. Lady on horseback, reverse of previous figure.

Figure 31.28. Gentleman on horseback, with a dog, with bocage. Possibly made by Hall. H: 7.7". The bocage leaves and flowers are suggestive of Hall. Pairs with the following equestrienne. Price D, pair.

12

Figure 31.29. Lady on horseback, with a dog, with bocage. Possibly made by Hall. H: 7.7". Pairs with the previous equestrian. Price D, pair.

Figure 31.30. Lady on horseback, with bocage. H: ~7.7". Price C.

Figure 31.31. Gentleman on horseback, with bocage. H: 7.5". A very unusual base and combination of bocage leaves and flowers. The same bocage leaves and flowers occur on figure 103.2 and Volume 3, figure 137.6. Price D. *Brighton and Hove Museums.*

Figure 31.32. Gentleman on horseback, with bocage. Attributed to Blue Group. H: ~6.8". The bocage flowers are gilded, a feature noted on one other figure from this Group. Price C. *The Moore Collection.*

Figure 31.33. Gentleman on horseback, reverse of previous figure. Blue Group figures are sometimes unpainted on the back. *The Moore Collection.*

Figure 31.34. Hunt servant on horse. H: 8". The man is dressed as a jockey, but his saddle and horn indicate he is a hunt servant. Decorated with both under-glaze and enamel colors. Price D. *Brighton and Hove Museums.*

Figure 31.35. Small toper on horseback. H: 5.7". The base is decorated in colored glazes. The seam through the horse's body has opened. Horses of this form on similar bases occur most commonly in under-glaze colors. Price C. *Bonhams.*

Figure 31.36. Military figure on horseback. H: 22". This very large figure on slender legs presented firing challenges, and the torso has buckled. Note a block placed under a rear leg and early tinker's repairs to the legs. Price G. *John Howard; www.antiquepottery.co.uk.*

Figure 31.37. Cossack soldier. Possibly made by Enoch Wood/Wood & Caldwell. H: 13". Gilding and silver luster are on the scabbard. *The Brave Cossack,* the first full-scale hippodrama, was performed at Astley's in 1807 and again in 1812, and perhaps it inspired this figure. Price E. *Brighton and Hove Museums.*

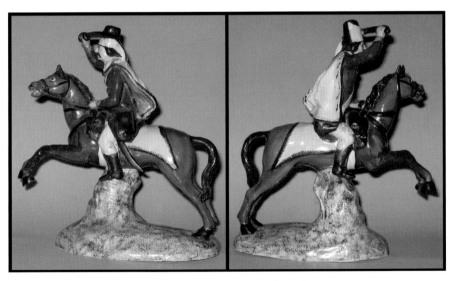

Figure 31.38. Cossack soldier. H: 10.5". Like the previous Cossack, probably portrays an equestrian from *The Brave Cossack,* staged while Russian Cossacks were fighting Napoleon. Price C. *John Howard; www.antiquepottery.co.uk.*

Figure 31.39. Cossack soldier. H: ~10.5". Like the previous Cossack, but mounted on a rectangular base with canted corners. This figure also is recorded decorated in silver luster. Price C. *Andrew Dando Antiques.*

32. Turks and Other Fairground Entertainers

Figure 32.1. Gentleman Turk. H: 5.5". One of the earliest enamel-painted figures, dating from circa 1775 and from the same molds as similar salt-glazed figures. Price F. *Jonathan Horne.*

Figure 32.2. Turk holding a basket, with bocage. H: 6.9". Price B.

Figure 32.3. Gentleman Turk. Attributed to "Sherratt." H: 4.4". Made without bocage. "Sherratt" made several other small figures, including musicians, on this base and to this scale. Price A.

Figure 32.4. Turk. H: 6.2". The base suggests that this figure was made in the eighteenth century. Made without bocage. Price A. *Aurea Carter Antiques.*

Figure 32.5. Turk. H: ~6". Made without bocage. Price A.

Figure 32.6. Turk. H: ~5.5". Made without bocage. Price A.

Figure 32.7. Gentleman Turk, with bocage. Attributed to Dudson. H: ~5.7". This Turk is unusual in that he is bearded. Pairs with the following lady Turk. Price A.

Figure 32.8. Lady Turk, with bocage. Attributed to Dudson. H: ~5.7". Pairs with the previous gentleman Turk and, like it, has a bocage that is specific to Dudson. Price A.

Figure 32.9. Turk, with bocage. H: ~5.7". Price A.

Figure 32.10. Lady Turk, with bocage. H: 5.7". Price A.

Figure 32.11. Lady Turk, reverse of previous example. The round flower stalks integral to the leaves are clearly visible.

Figure 32.12. Lady Turk, with bocage. H: ~5.7". Left side of bocage restored. Price A.

Figure 32.13. Lady and gentleman Turks, a pair, with bocages. H: 5.2". Price B. *Áurea Carter Antiques.*

Figure 32.14. Turk, with bocage. Attributed to Patriotic Group. H: 3.8". The base occurs only on other Patriotic Group figures, and the bocage fronds and painting style are consistent with the attribution. Price A.

Figure 32.15. Turk, reverse of previous figure. The six-leaflet bocage fronds occur on smaller Patriotic Group figures but are not specific to the Group.

Figure 32.16. Lady Turk, with bocage. Probably made by Enoch Wood. H: 3.8". The base and bocage are in the style of Enoch Wood. Price A.

Figure 32.17. Lady Turk, reverse of previous figure.

Figure 32.18. Gentleman and lady Turks, a pair with bocages. Possibly made by Enoch Wood. H: ~4". The bases and bocages (largely restored) are in the style of Enoch Wood. Price A.

Figure 32.19. Lady Turk. Possibly made by Enoch Wood. H: ~3.4". Made without bocage. Price A.

Figure 32.20. Gentleman Turk. H: 4". Pairs with the following lady. Made without bocage. Price A. *Collection of Michael J. Smith.*

Figure 32.21. Lady Turk. H: 4". Pairs with the previous gentleman. Made without bocage. Price A. *Collection of Michael J. Smith.*

Figure 32.22. Lady Turk. H: 3.6". Made without bocage. Price A. *The Bowes Museum, Barnard Castle.*

Figure 32.23. Lady Turk. H: ~3.5". Made without bocage. Price A.

Figure 32.24. Gentleman Turk. H: 5.5". Made without bocage. Price A. *Andrew Dando Antiques.*

Figure 32.25. Gentleman Turk. H: 5.5". Made without bocage. Price A. *Elinor Penna.*

Figure 32.26. Gentleman Turk. H: 5.5". Note the flowers on his hat. Made without bocage. Price A. *Peter Flemans.*

Figure 32.27. Lady Turk. Attributed to Dudson. H: ~5.5". The x-sprig at her feet establishes the attribution. Price A.

Figure 32.28. A pair of Turks. H: 4". Made without bocages. Price B.

Figure 32.29. Gentleman in Oriental attire, or perhaps a clown. H: 4". Three leaflets are attached to the leg in lieu of a bocage. Price A. *Image courtesy of The Potteries Museum & Art Gallery, Stoke-on-Trent, UK.*

Figure 32.30. Gentleman in Oriental attire. H: 4". Made without bocage. Price A.

Figure 32.31. Gentleman Turk, with bocage. Impressed "TITTENSOR". H ~6". These twelve-petalled bocage flowers are only on two other Tittensor figures and on Dale figures. Tittensor also made this figure decorated in under-glaze colors and with a bocage of a form only found on under-glaze Tittensor figures. Price A.

Figure 32.32. Exotically attired gentleman entertainer. H: ~6.3". Price A.

Figure 32.33. *Clown.* Attributed to Ralph Wood; impressed "6". H: 7.9". This figure form was first manufactured to represent winter by Lunéville, after a model by Paul Louis Cyfflé. Ralph Wood examples occur impressed "5," "6," or "74" and may be titled *Sloth* or *Clown.* Price A. *Aurea Carter Antiques.*

Figure 32.34. *Clown*. Attributed to Ralph Wood. H: 7.6". Like the previous figure but without an impressed number. Price A. *Elinor Penna*.

Figure 32.35. Puzzle jug with Turk, with "T. L. 1839" painted on it. H: 12.2". The small Turk protruding from the body of the jug is like that found on "Sherratt" menageries. Price C. *John Howard; www.antiquepottery.co.uk*.

Literature and Theater
33. Anthony and Cleopatra

Anthony and Cleopatra are the tragic lovers in William Shakespeare's *Anthony and Cleopatra*. Earthenware figures of Cleopatra derive from the marble statue of Ariadne in the Vatican, and a reduced-size plaster cast or bronze possibly assisted with their modeling. The statue of Ariadne has a snake bracelet entwined on the upper arm, but on earthenware figures of Cleopatra it is replaced with the asp that killed Cleopatra. The design source for the figure of Anthony has not been identified. Also recorded, but not shown, is a figure of Cleopatra impressed "NEALE & Co." It is styled much like other figures of Cleopatra, but Cleopatra's sandal has a heart-shaped clasp. This feature may help attribute unmarked examples.

Figure 33.1. Statue of Ariadne in the Vatican Museums. © *wknight94*.

Figure 33.2. Anthony. Attributed to Enoch Wood/Wood & Caldwell. L: ~12". The flowers on the base occur on marked Wood & Caldwell figures. Pairs with the next figure of Cleopatra. Price C, pair. *John Howard; www. antiquepottery.co.uk.*

Figure 33.4. Anthony. L: 12.5". Pairs with the following figure of Cleopatra. Price B, pair. *M. J. Meehan*.

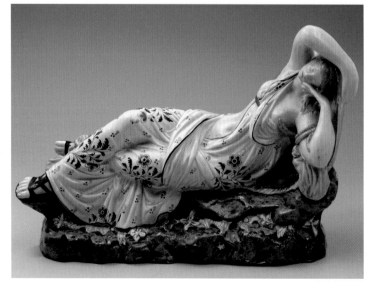

Figure 33.3. Cleopatra. Attributed to Enoch Wood/Wood & Caldwell. L: ~12". Pairs with the previous figure of Anthony. Price C, pair. *John Howard; www.antiquepottery.co.uk.*

Figure 33.5. Cleopatra. L: 12.7". Pairs with the previous figure of Anthony. Price B, pair. *M. J. Meehan.*

Figure 33.6. Cleopatra. L: 11". Note the particularly long snake around her arm. Price B. *John Howard; www.antiquepottery.co.uk.*

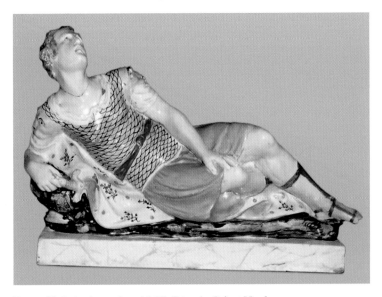

Figure 33.7. Anthony. L: ~11.5". Price A. *Robert Hawker.*

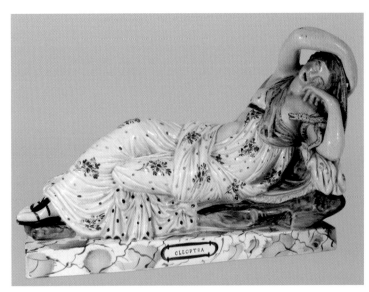

Figure 33.8. *CLEOPTRA.* Impressed "WEDGWOOD." L: 9.8". Price B. *Brighton and Hove Museums.*

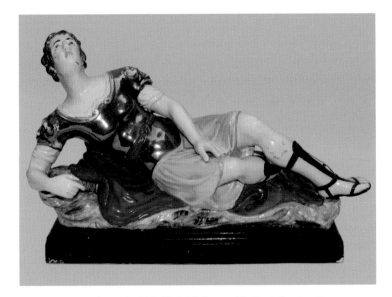

Figure 33.9. Anthony. L: 11", H: 7.2". Pairs with the following figure of Cleopatra. Price B, pair. *Collection of Arnold and Barbara Berlin.*

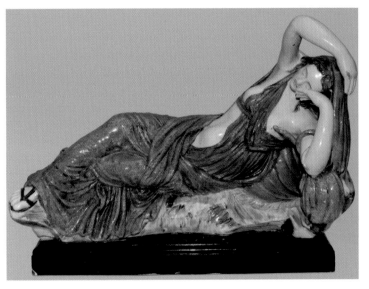

Figure 33.10. Cleopatra. L: 11", H: 9.1". Pairs with the previous figure of Anthony. The snake is especially short on this model. Price B, pair. *Collection of Arnold and Barbara Berlin.*

34. Ophelia

Ophelia is the tragic heroine of Shakespeare's *Hamlet*. Loved by Hamlet, Ophelia climbs into a willow tree, but a branch breaks, and Ophelia plunges into the brook beneath and drowns. Appropriately, the earthenware Ophelia has a willow branch wrapped around her. Creamware pairs of Ophelia and Hamlet, possibly made at Leeds and decorated in colored glazes, have been noted. In these, Hamlet too is draped in a willow branch. As yet, no enamel-painted Hamlet has been recorded. Also, a figure of a recumbent lady draped in a cloak, eyes closed, and clutching a flower in each hand, has been described as "possibly Ophelia."[1]

Figure 34.3. Ophelia. H: 13.8". Like the previous figure, but with a different base. The figures are probably from the same molds, but the faces and heads are painted quite differently. Price B. *Aurea Carter Antiques.*

Figure 34.1. Ophelia. H: 14.5". Note the flowers at Ophelia's feet. Unlike some other forms of this figure, the areas above both shoulders and to the right of the body are open. Price B.

Figure 34.2. Ophelia, reverse of previous figure.

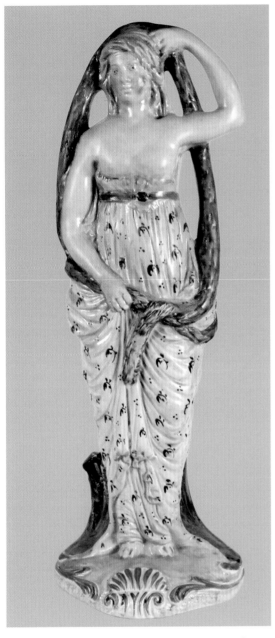

Figure 34.4. Ophelia. H: 12.9". Like the previous figure, but on a different base. The dress patterns are very similar. Price B. *Elinor Penna*.

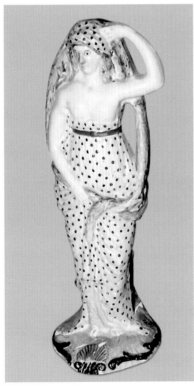

Figure 34.6. Ophelia. H: 13.2". The head closely resembles that on the previous figure of Ophelia, but there is no open space above the shoulders. Price A.

Figure 34.7. Ophelia. H: 12.3". Note the pink luster decoration. Unlike other examples in that there is no open space either above the shoulders or to the right of the body. Price B. *Elinor Penna*.

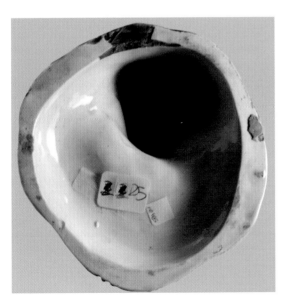

Figure 34.5. Ophelia, previous figure from beneath. The glazed rim of the base indicates that this figure was made without the square base present on the previous examples. Price B. *Elinor Penna*.

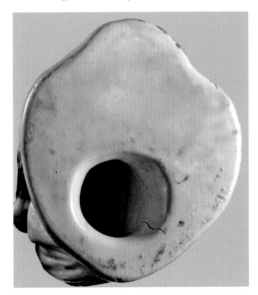

Figure 34.8. Ophelia, previous figure from beneath. *Elinor Penna*.

27

35. Falstaff

Sir John Falstaff is the rotund, cowardly knight in Shakespeare's *Henry IV, Part 1,* and *Henry IV, Part 2,* and in *The Merry Wives of Windsor.* The most common earthenware figure form shows Falstaff standing with his sword raised. Derby produced a similar porcelain model, circa 1770, and reissued it in the early 1800s. The figure derives from either the mezzotint or the painting by James McArdell depicting the actor James Quinn in the role of Sir John Falstaff in 1746 and 1747.

Falstaff appears in numerous contemporary engravings. Henry Bunbury's engraving of *Falstaff at Justice Shallow's Mustering his Recruits,* published in 1792, depicts Falstaff seated and may have inspired the rather unusual small seated figure shown in figure 35.10.

Mr. Quin in the Character of Sr. IOHN FALSTAFF.
London, Printed for Robt. Sayer, Map & Printseller, at No 53 in Fleet Street.

Figure 35.1. *Mr. Quinn in the Role of Sir John Falstaff* by James McArdell, published by Robert Sayer, circa 1760. © *Victoria and Albert Museum, London.*

Figure 35.2. Falstaff. Impressed "WOOD & CALDWELL". H: 8.8". On this model of Falstaff, the hand holding the sword is commonly restored or lost. Price A. *Wisbech & Fenland Museum.*

Figure 35.3. Falstaff, reverse of previous figure. Enoch Wood continued making this figure after the dissolution of his partnership with Caldwell, as evidenced by a partial figure among excavated Enoch Wood shards from the Burslem Old Town Hall site, circa 1820–30. *Wisbech & Fenland Museum*

Figure 35.4. Falstaff. Impressed "WOOD & CALDWELL". H: ~8.7". Price A.

Figure 35.5. Falstaff. Impressed "WOOD & CALDWELL". H: 8.7". Price A.

Figure 35.6. Falstaff. Impressed "WOOD & CALDWELL". H: 8.7". Silver luster was introduced commercially in 1805, so this figure was made after 1805 and before the dissolution of Wood & Caldwell in July 1818. Price A. *Brighton and Hove Museums.*

Figure 35.7. Falstaff. H: 8.4". This model of Falstaff differs from the Wood & Caldwell model, and the sword arm is not as exposed to damage. Price B. *Andrew Dando Antiques.*

Figure 35.8. Falstaff. H: ~8.2". Probably from the same manufactory as the previous figure. Note the elaborate pattern on the waistcoat. Price B. *Andrew Dando Antiques.*

Figure 35.9. Detail of *Falstaff at Justice Shallow's Mustering his Recruits,* by Henry Bunbury, published 1792.

Figure 35.10. Falstaff. H: 4.5". This model of Falstaff is uncommon. Price A.

36. Doctor Syntax

Figures of Doctor Syntax are inspired by Thomas Rowlandson's amusing aquatint illustrations of this traveling clergyman. William Combe wrote *The Schooolmaster's Tour* as a comic poem to accompany Rowlandson's illustrations, and it was published in serial form from 1809 to 1811. In 1812, a revised version (including thirty Rowlandson aquatints) was published as *The Tour of Doctor Syntax in Search of the Picturesque*. The volume was immensely popular, and *The Second Tour of Doctor Syntax in Search of Consolation* (1820) and *The Third Tour of Doctor Syntax in Search of a Wife* (1821) completed the trilogy. Other authors climbed on the Syntax bandwagon and published Syntax knock-offs. In the same vein, earthenware figures capitalized on the Doctor Syntax theme.

Figure 36.1. Detail of *Doctor Syntax Stopt by Highwaymen*, by Thomas Rowlandson, first published circa 1810.

Figure 36.2. *DR SYNTAX STOPPED BY HIGHWAYMEN*, with bocage. Attributed to Patriotic Group. H: 8.6". The titled plaque and the bocage support attribution. A very rare figure. Other recorded examples have lost the highwayman from the base. Price D.

Figure 36.3. Doctor Syntax playing cards with a gentleman, with bocage. Attributed to "Sherratt." H: 7.7". This group was inspired by—but does not resemble—Rowlandson's engraving of *Doctor Syntax at a Card Party*, from *The Third Tour of Doctor Syntax* (1821). Price D. *Brighton and Hove Museums.*

Figure 36.4. Doctor Syntax playing cards with a gentleman, with bocage. Attributed to "Sherratt." H: 7.9". Crude reproductions of this fine group abound. Price D.

Figure 36.5. Doctor Syntax playing cards with a gentleman, with bocage. Attributed to "Sherratt." H: ~7.9". The same base as the previous example, but the bocage fronds comprise fern leaflets rather than oak leaflets. Price D. *The Moore Collection.*

Figure 36.6. Doctor Syntax playing cards with a gentleman, with bocage. Attributed to "Sherratt." L: 8.5". Same base as the previous two examples but with anthemion bocage fronds. "Sherratt" painted rectangular tables to simulate wood grain, as seen here. Restored tables are seldom painted correctly. Price D. *Jonathan Horne.*

Figure 36.7. Doctor Syntax playing cards with a gentleman, with bocage. Attributed to "Sherratt." H: 6.9". The base is specific to "Sherratt." The anthemion bocage fronds are as on the previous example. Price C.

Figure 36.8. Doctor Syntax playing cards with a gentleman, with bocage. Attributed to "Sherratt." H: ~8". A typical "Sherratt" base and bocage. Possible restoration to the gentleman's hat/head. Price B. *Collection of Arnold and Barbara Berlin.*

Figure 36.9. Doctor Syntax playing cards with a gentleman. Attributed to "Sherratt." H: 6.5". Made without bocage. Price C. *Collection of Michael J. Smith.*

Figure 36.10. Doctor Syntax playing cards with a gentleman, within an arbor. H: 6.3". Other groups (weddings, musicians, performing animals, dame schools) occur within this arbor. Price C.

Figure 36.11. Doctor Syntax playing cards with a gentleman, within an arbor. H: 6". A rare variant. The base of the arbor is painted green, whereas most arbors have vermicular decoration. Compared to the previous example, the figures are from different molds and have switched positions. Price C. *Brighton and Hove Museums.*

Figure 36.12. Doctor Syntax playing cards with a gentleman, with bocage. H: ~6.5". A rare small group with the same bocage and from the same pot bank as the following example. Price C.

Figure 36.13. Doctor Syntax playing cards with a gentleman, with bocage. H: 6.5". The unusual bocage leaves are only otherwise recorded on this and the previous example and on a small courtship group (Vol. 4, fig. 138.16). Price C. *The William Herbert and Nancy Hunt Collection.*

Figure 36.14. Detail of the base of the previous Doctor Syntax group. *The William Herbert and Nancy Hunt Collection.*

Figure 36.15. *DR SYNTAX.* Doctor Syntax carried by a woman, with bocage. H: 5.9". The source print is *Doctor Syntax Landing at Calais.* It illustrates *Doctor Syntax in Paris* (1820), an illustrated narrative mimicking Rowlandson's and Combe's work. Price B. *Collection of Arnold and Barbara Berlin.*

Figure 36.16. Detail of *Dr. Syntax Tied to a Tree by Highwaymen*, first published circa 1810.

Figure 36.17. Doctor Syntax tied to a tree. H: ~5". The figure derives from the previous illustration of *Dr. Syntax Tied to a Tree by Highwaymen.* Made without bocage. Price B.

Figure 36.18. Doctor Syntax tied to a tree. Attributed to Gray Base Group. H: 5.5". Made without bocage. Price B. *Collection of Arnold and Barbara Berlin.*

DR. SYNTAX

DR. SYNTAX

Figure 36.19. *DR SYNTAX, DR SYNTAX.* Two figures of Doctor Syntax tied to a tree, each with bocage. H: ~5.6". From the same figure molds. Price B each.

Figure 36.20. *DR SYNTAX, DR SYNTAX.* Reverse of the previous two figures of Doctor Syntax tied to a tree. Each is made with only two bocage fronds. Note the rope binding Syntax to the tree.

Figure 36.22. Doctor Syntax playing the violin. Attributed to the Gray Base Group. H: 6". Possibly after the illustration on the frontispiece of the final book in the Syntax trilogy. Made without bocage. The base has a yellow tinge, as is sometimes seen on Gray Base examples. Price B. *The William Herbert and Nancy Hunt Collection.*

Figure 36.21. Detail of the frontispiece of *The Third Tour of Doctor Syntax in Search of a Wife*, first published in 1821.

Figure 36.23. Detail of *Dr. Syntax Reading His Tour*, first published circa 1810.

Figure 36.24. *DR SYNTAX* (title faintly impressed on base). Dr. Syntax reading his tour. H: 6". After the illustration of the same subject, first published circa 1810. Price B. *Brighton and Hove Museums.*

Figure 36.26. Detail of *Dr. Syntax Losing His Way,* first published circa 1810.

Figure 36.25. Dr. Syntax reading his tour. Attributed to Gray Base Group. H: ~5.5". After the illustration on this theme, previously shown. Price B. *Woolley and Wallis Salisbury Salerooms Ltd.*

Figure 36.27. Doctor Syntax Losing His Way. H: 6". After the illustration of this subject first published circa 1810. Made without bocage. Price C.

Figure 36.28. Doctor Syntax. H: 5.9". With losses. Made without bocage. An unusual figure portraying Syntax in an undetermined role. Price A. *Martyn Edgell Antiques Ltd.*

37. Tam O'Shanter and Souter Johnny

Robert Burns's *Tam O'Shanter* (1791) was enormously popular in the early nineteenth century. The poem tells of Tam spending an evening with his drinking companion Souter Johnny, and, heading home in a drunken haze, he encounters witches and warlocks, with comic results. In 1828, James Thom (1802–1850), working as a gravestone mason, secured a commission to cut life-sized figures of Tam O'Shanter and Souter Johnny. Thom modeled the statues as composites of various local characters. The statues toured from 1828 to 1830 and were exhibited in London in 1829 to critical acclaim. The exhibitions were so successful that cast makers quickly produced painted plaster replicas of the figures in miniature sizes. Also, sketches of the statues were sold at the exhibitions, and print makers capitalized on the popular theme. A syndicate ordered a set of four statues—to include the landlord and landlady from the poem—and, to Thom's rage, these were exhibited in Liverpool and Birmingham in 1829. Earthenware figures of Tam and Souter Johnny cannot predate 1828, and all derive from Thom's sculptures or an accurate intermediary source.

Thom carved five sets of statues in the United Kingdom before sailing to America in 1835. One of these sets was carved in 1830 for the Earl of Cassillis, and it included a small tripod table. The earl placed his statues in a faux ale house in his garden. The "Sherratt" group of Tam and Souter Johnny in figure 37.9 incorporates a little tripod table, so it was probably made from around 1830, after an illustration of this set of statues.

TAM O'SHANTER & SOUTER JOHNNY.

The Souter tould his queerest stories
The Landlord's laugh was ready chorus.
The storm without might rair and rustle.
Tam didna mind the storm a whistle.

Figure 37.2. *Tam O'Shanter & Souter Johnny*, published circa 1830.

Figure 37.1. James Thom's life-sized stone statues of Tam O'Shanter and Souter Johnny, one of the many pairs that Thom chiseled from 1828. *Burns National Heritage Park.*

Figure 37.3. Tam O'Shanter and Souter Johnny. Attributed to "Sherratt." H: 6.9" (L), 6.5" (R). These figures also occur together on a single base (fig. 37.10). Price C.

Figure 37.4. Souter Johnny and Tam O'Shanter. Attributed to "Sherratt." H: 6.7" (L), 7" (R). Like the previous pair but on differently painted "Sherratt" bases. Price B. *Peter Flemans.*

Figure 37.5. Souter Johnny and Tam O'Shanter. H: 5.5". Price A.

Figure 37.6. Tam O'Shanter and Souter Johnny. H: 5.3". Price B. *Image courtesy of The Potteries Museum & Art Gallery, Stoke-on-Trent, UK.*

Figure 37.7. Tam O'Shanter and Souter Johnny. H: 15.2" (L), 14.7" (R). Note the large size. Price D. *Collection of Michael J. Smith.*

Figure 37.9. *TAM O'SHANTER SOUTER JOHNNY.* Attributed to "Sherratt." H: 7.3". The figures also each occur on separate bases, previously shown. Probably inspired by Thom's set of statues carved to include a small table, seen in the previous print. Price C.

The Landlady and Tam grew gracious,
Wi' favours secret, sweet, and precious:
The Souter tauld his queerest stories,
The Landlord's laugh was ready chorus.

FROM THE CELEBRATED FIGURES, TAM O'SHANTER, SOUTER JOHNNY, THE LANDLORD AND LANDLADY. J. THOM. *sculp.*

Figure 37.8. *From the Celebrated Figures, Tam O'Shanter, Souter Johnny, The Landlord and Landlady,* published circa 1835.

38. Charlotte at the Tomb of Werther

The Sorrows of Young Werther, a German novella by Johann Wolfgang von Goethe published in 1774, tells of Werther, who kills himself when he cannot have Charlotte, the woman he loves. The book was first published in English in 1779. In 1785, a tragic adaptation by Frederick Reynolds opened on the London stage. Meissen and Derby modeled Charlotte weeping for Werther in the 1780s, and the first Staffordshire figures, some looking like the Derby models, were probably made in this period. Although Charlotte buries Werther under a linden tree and there is no mention of ashes, figures portray her clutching a funeral urn.

Figure 38.2. Charlotte at the tomb of Werther. H: 9". Made without bocage. Price A. *The Bowes Museum, Barnard Castle.*

Figure 38.1. Charlotte at the tomb of Werther, with bocage. Attributed to Enoch Wood. H: 10.2". Impressed "10" and painted "3" beneath. The unusual bocage matches excavated Enoch Wood shards, and the numbers beneath the base are also typical of this pot bank. Price B.

Figure 38.3. Charlotte at the tomb of Werther. H: 9.2". Made without bocage. Price A. *Brighton and Hove Museums.*

Figure 38.4. Charlotte at the tomb of Werther. H: 9". Made without bocage. Price A. *Barbara Gair; www.castle-antiques.com.*

39. Cymon and Iphigenia

Cymon is the hero of *The Decameron*, a novella set in Cyprus and written around 1350 by Giovanni Boccaccio. The narrative tells of Cymon who, deemed a dolt by his aristocratic father, is sent to live and work with his father's slaves in the countryside. In this environment, Cymon becomes increasingly coarse. One day, Cymon comes upon highborn Iphigenia, slumbering in a field. He is so smitten by her beauty that his noble bearing surfaces, and his father reinstates him. Iphigenia is promised to another, but this tale of wars and abduction in the name of love ends happily with Cymon and Iphigenia united for life. In 1700, John Dryden published his *Fables, Ancient and Modern*, containing the story as a poem. The figure of Cymon (usually *Simon*, if titled) is said to be modeled from the figure Paul Louis Cyfflé made for Lunéville, but a similar Strasbourg porcelain figure circa 1760 may predate it.

Figure 39.2. *SIMON* (title faintly impressed on front of base). Probably made by Ralph Wedgwood. H: 9.5". Made without bocage. A marked Wedgwood figure of Simon is recorded, and the titling is typical of Wedgwood figures. Pairs with the following Iphigenia. Price B. *Wisbech & Fenland Museum.*

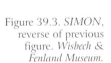

Figure 39.1. *Iphigenia, Simon.* Attributed to Ralph Wood; Simon impressed "96". H: ~9". Made without bocage. Simon is also found impressed "135" and "97" (to be added to list in Vol. 1, Chap. 14). Iphigenia may be impressed "96" or "136". Price B.

Figure 39.3. *SIMON*, reverse of previous figure. *Wisbech & Fenland Museum.*

Figure 39.4. *IPHIGENIA* (title faintly impressed on front of base). Probably made by Ralph Wedgwood. H: 8.8". The titling is typical of Wedgwood figures. Pairs with the previous Simon. Price B. *Wisbech & Fenland Museum.*

Figure 39.5. *IPHIGENIA*, reverse of previous figure. *Wisbech & Fenland Museum.*

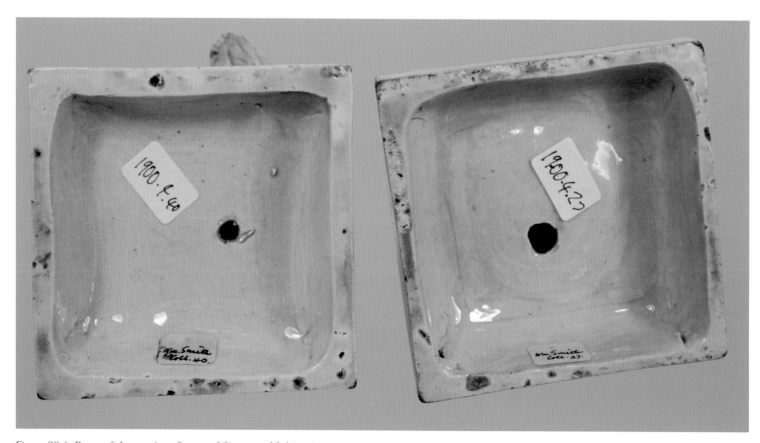

Figure 39.6. Bases of the previous figures of Simon and Iphigenia, probably made by Wedgwood. *Wisbech & Fenland Museum*

Figure 39.7. Iphigenia and Simon. H: 8" (L), 8.5" (R). Price B. *Nick Burton.*

Figure 39.8. Iphigenia and Simon, reverse of previous pair. *Nick Burton.*

Figure 39.9. Simon, with bocage. H: 8.8". This is the only recorded example of this figure. Price A. *Aurea Carter Antiques.*

Figure 39.10. Simon, reverse of previous figure showing the unusual bocage (with losses). The bocage fronds are as on figure 155.82 in Volume 4. *Aurea Carter Antiques.*

40. Grecian & Daughter

Figure groups of *GRECIAN & DAUGHTER* portray the story of Pero and her father, Cimon. Cimon is jailed and sentenced to death by starvation, but Pero breastfeeds him to keep him alive. She is detected, and her selflessness earns Cimon's release. The Roman historian Valerius Maximus told this tale in his *Nine Books of Memorable Acts and Sayings of the Ancient Romans,* circa 30 C.E. A fresco in Pompeii depicts the scene, and Baroque artists popularized the theme. Later, Peter Paul Rubens painted Pero feeding the chained Cimon. By 1765, Chelsea had modeled a figure group of Cimon and Pero.

In the eighteenth century, Arthur Murphy lifted the plot of Cimon and Pero to provide a stage role for the ailing actor Mr. Barry. His play, titled *The Grecian Daughter,* was first performed at Drury Lane in February 1772, with Mr. and Mrs. Barry in the roles of Evander and Euphrasia, the Grecian and his daughter respectively. The play ran on provincial stages and on the London stage until about 1815. It was revived in 1830 for Miss Fanny Kemble, and that revival probably inspired the earthenware figure groups, all examples of which are in the "Sherratt" style. Not shown here is a group on a "Sherratt" brown table base. Unusually, a mounded "Sherratt" rainbow base was then placed atop that table base, in lieu of the naturalistic mound that is normally present.

Figure 40.1. *GRECIAN & DAUGHTER.* Attributed to "Sherratt." H: 9.8". The base, the turret-type spill vases, and the bocage are typical of "Sherratt." Price C. *John Howard; www.antiquepottery.co.uk.*

Figure 40.2. *GRECIAN & DAUGHTER.* Probably attributable to "Sherratt." H: 10.7". Perhaps a little later than the previous example and from the same molds. Price C. *John Howard; www.antiquepottery.co.uk.*

41. Poor Maria

The figure of Poor Maria derives from Laurence Sterne's *A Sentimental Journey through France and Italy*, published in 1768. Sterne's work reads, "I discovered poor Maria sitting under a poplar—she was sitting with her elbow in her lap, and her head leaning on one side within her hand ... She was dress'd in white, and much as my friend had described her, except that her hair hung loose, which before was twisted within a silk net. She had superadded likewise to her jacket, a pale green ribband, which fell across her shoulder to the waist; at the end of which hung her pipe. Her goat had been as faithless as her lover; and she had got a little dog in lieu of him, which she had kept tied by a string to her girdle."

In 1775, the character of Maria was portrayed for the first time in a painting by Mary Bertrand at the Royal Academy, but the most well-known depiction—and the source of the figure—is Joseph Wright of Derby's *Maria with her dog Silvio*, 1781. The figure can occur paired with Agrippina with the ashes of Germanicus (Vol. 4, ch. 157).

Figure 41.1. *Maria with her dog Silvio*, Joseph Wright of Derby, 1781.

Figure 41.2. Poor Maria, with spill vase and bocage. H: ~7.5". Pairs with a figure of Agrippina (Vol. 4, fig. 157.2). Each has a bocage, but no other example of either figure with bocage is recorded. Price B. *Andrew Dando Antiques.*

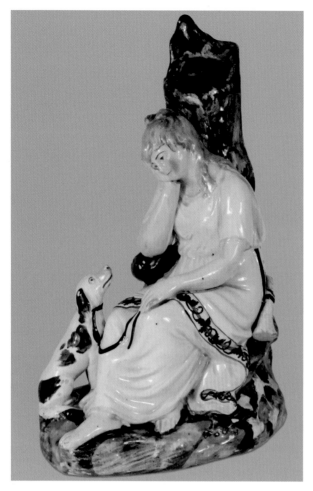

Figure 41.3. Poor Maria, with spill vase. H: 7.5". Price A. *Brighton and Hove Museums.*

Figure 41.4. Poor Maria, with spill vase. H: 7.8". Incised "WL1804" beneath. Companion to Agrippina (Vol. 4, figs. 157.4–5), incised "1804". Price B. *Image courtesy of The Potteries Museum & Art Gallery, Stoke-on-Trent, UK.*

Figure 41.5. Poor Maria, previous figure. *Image courtesy of The Potteries Museum & Art Gallery, Stoke-on-Trent, UK.*

Figure 41.6. Detail of the floral sprigs on the previous figure. *Image courtesy of The Potteries Museum & Art Gallery, Stoke-on-Trent, UK.*

42. Rinaldo and Armida

The characters of Rinaldo and Armida are from Torquato Tasso's poem *Gerusalemme Liberata* (*Jerusalem Delivered*), circa 1581. The poem's tale is one of love and heroism in battle during the First Crusade (1096–1099). The sorceress Armida tries to kill the knight Rinaldo, but instead falls in love with him and bewitches him. By 1600, the poem had been translated into English, and it was to remain popular in England into the nineteenth century, inspiring music, plays, and numerous paintings. Notably, in 1711, Handel's opera *Rinaldo* was London's first Italian opera.

Van Dyck's painting *Rinaldo and Armida* (1629) and the Derby figure of the late 1770s show Rinaldo with his eyes closed. These portrayals probably depict the moment at which Armida, filled with hatred for Rinaldo, finds him asleep, but, overwhelmed by his beauty, is unable to destroy him. In earthenware groups, however, Rinaldo's eyes are open and Armida dangles a laurel crown over his head, perhaps showing the moment when she tries to entice him with her charms.

Figure 42.2. *RINALDO & ARMIDA*. Attributed to Lakin & Poole. H: ~9.4". Price C.

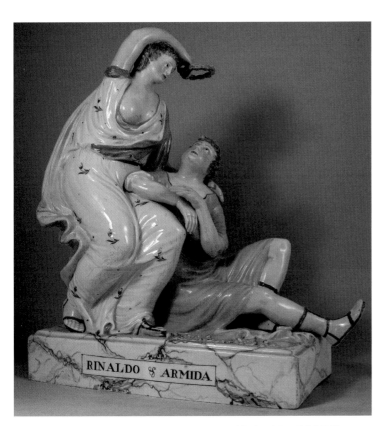

Figure 42.1. *RINALDO & ARMIDA*. Impressed "LAKIN & POOLE". H: ~9.4". Price D.

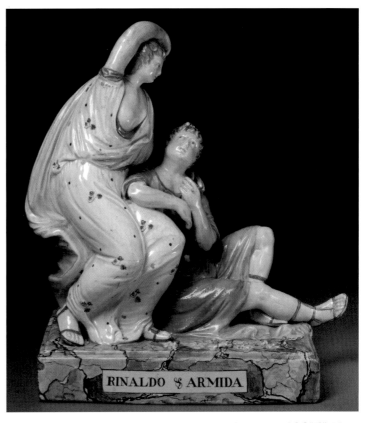

Figure 42.3. *RINALDO & ARMIDA*. Impressed "LAKIN & POOLE". H: 9.5". The base is more brightly marbled than is usual on Lakin examples. Price D. © *Victoria and Albert Museum, London.*

43. Hudibras

In Samuel Butler's satirical poem *Hudibras*, written between 1663 and 1678 and set in England's Civil War, Hudibras is a goofy, zealous knight. In 1721 and 1726, William Hogarth illustrated new editions of the poem that were to remain popular for another century. The figure of Hudibras was probably first made by Ralph Wood after Hogarth's engraving *Hudibras, Triumphant*.

Figure 43.1. *Hudibras, Triumphant,* published by G. & I. Robinson, 1802.

Figure 43.2. Hudibras. Attributed to Ralph Wood; impressed "41". H: 11.5". This figure also occurs impressed "42". Price C. *Image courtesy of The Potteries Museum & Art Gallery, Stoke-on-Trent, UK.*

Figure 43.3. Hudibras, reverse of previous example. *Image courtesy of The Potteries Museum & Art Gallery, Stoke-on-Trent, UK.*

Figure 43.4. Hudibras. Probably made by Ralph Wood. H: ~11.5".
The painting atop the base is typical of Ralph Wood. Price B.
Andrew Dando Antiques.

Figure 43.5. Hudibras. Probably made by Ralph Wood. H: 11.8".
The base is painted in the style of Ralph Wood. Price B. *Woolley
and Wallis Salisbury Salerooms Ltd.*

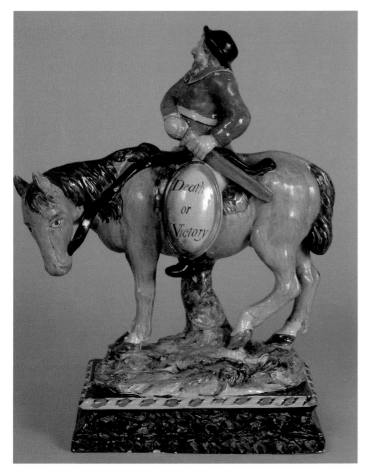

Figure 43.6. Hudibras. "Death or Victory" painted on the shield.
Probably made by Ralph Wood. H: 11.2". Titling in this script occurs
on Ralph Wood figures painted in a murkier palette. Price B. *Andrew
Dando Antiques.*

Figure 43.7. *Hudibras.* "Death or Victory" painted on the shield.
H: 12.7". St. George and the dragon and the Vicar and Moses
stand on bases formed and titled in the same manner. Price B.
The William Herbert and Nancy Hunt Collection.

44. Jobson and Nell

Jobson, a wife-beating cobbler, and his sweet wife, Nell, were the central characters of *The Devil to Pay, or the Wives Metamorphos'd,* a ballad opera written by Charles Coffey. This comic performance opened on the London stage in 1731. Modified, it remained popular in the nineteenth century and it was staged at Covent Garden in 1828. Figures of Jobson and Nell occur in two sizes (around six to seven inches and thirteen to fourteen inches) and were made into the twentieth century. All known examples are made without bocages, with the exception of the small model shown in figure 44.15.

Figure 44.1. Nell and Jobson. H: 6.5". Price A. *Andrew Dando Antiques.*

Figure 44.2. Nell and Jobson. H: 6.4" (L), 6.9" (R). The modeling of the faces is distinctive, and this pair closely resembles a marked pair made by the Bramelds at the Swinton Pottery and impressed "BRAMELD+4". Price A. *Eileen and Robert Carde.*

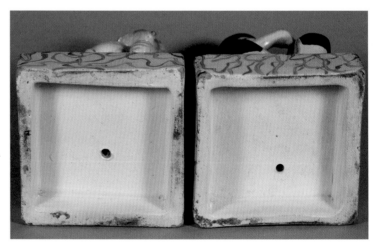

Figure 44.3. Nell and Jobson, bases of previous pair. *Eileen and Robert Carde.*

Figure 44.4. Nell and Jobson. H: 6.7" (L), 6" (R). Attributed to Enoch Wood. Both impressed "27" beneath. Price A. *Wisbech & Fenland Museum.*

Figure 44.7. Nell and Jobson. H: 13.1" (L), 13.5" (R). This pair resembles the previous pair, but is very much larger. Price B. *Image courtesy of The Potteries Museum & Art Gallery, Stoke-on-Trent, UK.*

Figure 44.5. Detail of previous figures of Jobson and Nell. He has a small dog beneath his chair, and she has a small cat beneath hers. *Wisbech & Fenland Museum.*

Figure 44.8. Nell and Jobson. H: 5.8" (L), 6.3" (R). Price A. *Image courtesy of The Potteries Museum & Art Gallery, Stoke-on-Trent, UK.*

Figure 44.6. The bases of the previous pair of figures. Both bases are impressed "27" beneath and are formed in a manner consistent with an Enoch Wood attribution.

Figure 44.9. *NELL, JOBSON*. Possibly attributable to Box Title Group. H: 6.3" (L), 6.6" (R). A small animal peeps out from beneath each stool, as is typical of Nell and Jobson models. Price B. *Eileen and Robert Carde.*

Figure 44.10. *JOBSON, NELL*. Both impressed "HALL". H: ~6.5". Hall is best remembered for figures of Jobson and Nell, but marked examples are uncommon. Price B.

Figure 44.11. Nell and Jobson. H: 6" (L), 6.3" (R). Price A.

Figure 44.12. Jobson. H: 7.3". Price A. *Whitehall Antiques, Chapel Hill, North Carolina.*

Figure 44.13. Jobson, side of previous figure showing the small animal beneath the stool. Note the black whisker-like design painted on the sides of the base. *Whitehall Antiques, Chapel Hill, North Carolina.*

Figure 44.14. Nell and Jobson. H: 6.3". Bases with the same distinctive decoration occur on New Marriage Act and Gretna Green wedding groups (Vol. 4, chap. 139). Price B. *Woolley and Wallis Salisbury Salerooms Ltd.*

Figure 44.15. Jobson and Nell, with bocages. H: ~5". Price B.

45. Jim Crow

In America around 1828, Thomas Dartmouth Rice (1808–1860), a prop man and small-part actor, performed between acts a shuffling, jiggling dance to the tune of a slave work song. The routine cruelly parodied the crippled movements of a slave named Jim Crow, who worked in the stables behind the theatre. Rice performed his Jim Crow routine in blackface, thus creating a stereotype for black minstrelsy that quickly became wildly popular. His debut as Jim Crow in London in 1836 was so successful that other plays were adapted to include a Jim Crow role, and Rice and Jim Crow became international sensations. People of all classes capered to the ditty, and printed images of Jim Crow proliferated. Figures of Jim Crow date no earlier than circa 1835 and are uncommon.

Figure 45.1. *JIM CROW,* published by Hodgson, London, and Turner & Fisher, New York and Philadelphia, n.d.

Figure 45.2. *JIM CROW.* Attributed to "Sherratt." H: 6.8". Price B. *Andrew Dando Antiques.*

Figure 45.3. *JAM CROW.* H: 6". The name "Jim" is an American contraction of "James," and ignorance of it probably caused it to be misspelled on this figure. Price B. *John Howard; www.antiquepottery.co.uk.*

Figure 45.4. Jim Crow. H: 6.3". Price B. *Andrew Dando Antiques.*

46. Grimaldi

Joseph Grimaldi (1779–1837) debuted at Sadler's Wells at three years of age and matured into the greatest clown of his day. He staged a final benefit performance in March 1828, on the very stage used for his debut. The earthenware figure of Grimaldi, known only from three examples in museums, matches Enoch Wood figure fragments of circa 1828 excavated from St. Paul's Church, Burslem. The figure possibly derives from a print, and that design source may also have inspired the similar Derby model of the same period.

Figure 46.1. *Mr. Grimaldi as Clown, in the Popular New Pantomime of Mother Goose*, published by S. D. De Wilde, February 1807.

Figure 46.2. Grimaldi. Attributed to Enoch Wood. H: 5.6". Reproductions of this fine figure abound. Price C. *Brighton and Hove Museums.*

47. Harlequin and Columbine

Commedia dell'arte, a theater form characterized by masked performers, originated in Europe in the fourteenth century. In the early 1700s in Britain, *commedia dell'arte* evolved into a comic adaptation known as harlequinade. By 1800, harlequinade had become a goofy, slapstick affair, and the lovers Harlequin and Columbine were its pivotal characters. In those days, an evening at the theater featured a mix of dramas and pantomimes, and a clownish harlequinade based on the pantomime was a nice finishing touch to the performance. Harlequin's mischievous, bawdy antics made him a lively addition to the stage, and he—and Columbine, to a lesser degree—enlivened the English stage into the Victorian era.

In the 1730s, Meissen made the first ceramic portrayals of Harlequin and Columbine, after engravings of *commedia dell'arte* characters. English porcelain factories followed suit, using both engravings and Meissen prototypes to influence their designs. Derby made Harlequin with a black mask from around 1770. Staffordshire figures of Harlequin and Columbine closely resemble Derby porcelain forms.

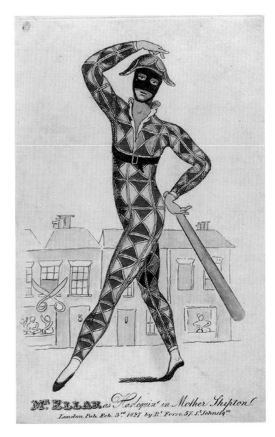

Figure 47.1. *Mr. Ellar as Harlequin in Mother Shipton*, published by R. Forse, February 1827.

Figure 47.2. Harlequin. H: ~5.5". Crude modern copies of this figure can be found. Made without bocage. Price B. *John Howard; www. antiquepottery.co.uk.*

Figure 47.3. Harlequin, with bocage. H: ~5.5". Price B. *Martyn Edgell Antiques Ltd.*

Figure 47.4. Harlequin, with bocage. H: ~5.5". Price B.

Figure 47.5. Harlequin, with bocage. H: ~5.5". Price B.

Figure 47.6. Harlequin, with bocage. H: ~5.5". Price B.

Figure 47.7. Harlequin, with bocage. H: ~5.5". Price B.

Figure 47.8. Columbine. Possibly made by Enoch Wood. H: ~5.5". Made without bocage. The base and the leaf on the stump would not be inconsistent with an Enoch Wood attribution. Price A.

Figure 47.9. Columbine. Possibly made by Enoch Wood. H: 5.5". Made without bocage. Price A. *Elinor Penna.*

Figure 47.10. Columbine, with bocage. H: 4.3". These three-leaflet fronds occur on other finely made figures, as yet unclassified. Price A. *Michael Goodacre.*

Figure 47.11. *Columbine*, reverse of previous figure. *Michael Goodacre.*

48. Little Jockey

Youth, Love, & Folly, a comic opera in two acts by William Dimond and Michael Kelly, opened at the Theatre Royal, Drury Lane, circa 1805. Notable for the role of a female actress disguised as a jockey named Arinette, the play was subsequently dubbed *The Little Jockey*. The actress Maria Foote was beloved in the role of Arinette or the Little Jockey, and the print of *Miss Foote as the Little Jockey* is probably the design source for the figure.

Figure 48.1. *Miss Foote as the Little Jockey*, published by O. Hodgson, n.d.

Figure 48.2. The Little Jockey. H: 6.9". A rare figure. Victorian versions are more common. Price B. © *Victoria and Albert Museum, London.*

49. Maria Malibran

Maria Malibran (1808–1836) was the world's first diva. Born into a renowned Spanish musical family and named Maria Garcia, she debuted in London in 1825 and toured Europe and America thereafter. As a mezzo-soprano of extraordinary vocal range and power, she earned international accolades and adoration. In 1826, she married the Frenchman Eugene Malibran, but the marriage was short-lived. In 1836, Miss Malibran sustained permanent head injuries when she fell off a horse. Thereafter, she performed a handful of times before collapsing on the stage in Manchester in September 1836 and dying days later.

Figures of Maria Malibran are based on an engraving for the *Dramatic Magazine* after A. M. Huffman by J. Rogers. Only two figures of Maria Malibran are recorded. In addition to the figure shown, a figure (possibly from the same molds) titled *MALIBRAN* occurs on a "Sherratt" base.[1] This "Sherratt" figure of Miss Malibran uses the same molds as the "Sherratt" figure titled *HER MAJESTY QUEEN VICTORIA* (fig. 66.1). Maria Malibran died shortly before Victoria came to the throne, so the figure of Malibran was conveniently reused to portray the young uncrowned queen.

Figure 49.1. *Mme. Malibran Garcia*, by J. Rogers after A. M. Huffman, n.d.

Figure 49.2. Maria Malibran. H: 7.6". Price C.
© *Fitzwilliam Museum, Cambridge.*

50. Broom Lady

Lucia Elizabeth Vestris (1797–1856), better known as Madame Vestris, was an English actress whose appearance and voice brought her acclaim on the English stage. In particular, her remarkable legs ensured her popularity in breeches roles. In 1826, Madame Vestris popularized the song *Buy a Broom*, which she sang on the London stage attired as a Bavarian broom seller. Engravings of her in this role inspired Staffordshire and Derby figures.

In 1826, Madame Vestris partnered with the great comedian John Liston. Dressed alike, they sang *Buy a Broom* together on the stage of the Theatre Royal Haymarket, and figures of a beefy broom lady portray Liston in his Broom Lady roll (figs. 50.9–10). A print showing this performance (fig. 50.8) may have influenced this figure model's design.

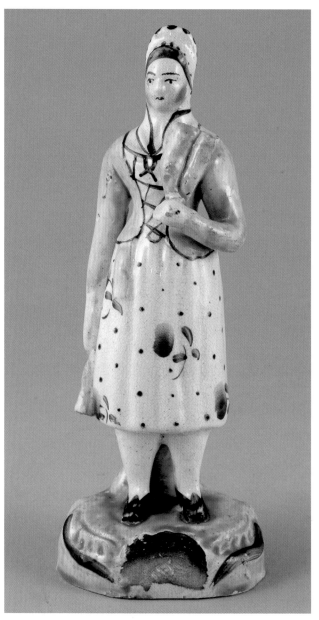

Figure 50.1. Madame Vestris as Broom Lady. H: ~6". This unusual base also occurs on other figures (Vol. 4, figs. 147.27–29). Price A. *Andrew Dando Antiques.*

Figure 50.2. Madame Vestris as Broom Lady. H: 6.1". A circle within a circle is impressed beneath. Price A.

Figure 50.3. Madame Vestris as Broom Lady, earthenware (L) and Derby porcelain (R). H: ~6.2". Possibly made by Enoch Wood (L). The earthenware figure is very like the porcelain example and similarly has an elaborately gilded dress pattern. Price A. *Andrew Dando Antiques.*

Figure 50.4. Madame Vestris as Broom Lady. H: 6.2". Possibly made by Enoch Wood. Like the previous example but painted in the more modest manner typical of earthenware. Price A. *Andrew Dando Antiques.*

Figure 50.5. Madame Vestris as Broom Lady. Attributed to "Sherratt." H: 5.8". Price A.

Figure 50.6. Madame Vestris as Broom Lady. Attributed to "Sherratt." H: 5.6". Like the previous example but painted differently. Price A. *Peter Flemans.*

Figure 50.7. Madame Vestris as Broom Lady. H: ~5.4". Price A.

Figure 50.8. *Mr. Liston & Madme. Vestris In the Duet of Buy a Broom*,
published by G. Humphrey, Nov. 1826. © *Trustees of the British Museum.*

Figure 50.9. *BY
A BROOM.* H:
6.4". Mr. Liston
as the Broom
Lady. Price A.
© *Victoria and
Albert Museum,
London.*

Figure 50.10. *BY
A BROOM.* H:
6.4". Mr. Liston
as the Broom
Lady. Price A.
*Image courtesy
of The Potteries
Museum & Art
Gallery, Stoke-on-
Trent, UK.*

51. Paul Pry

John Liston (1776–1846) was the leading comic actor of his day. His most memorable role was that of Paul Pry in the play *Paul Pry,* which was written by John Poole and opened at the Haymarket Theatre on September 13, 1825. Paul Pry was an interfering busybody. His trademark umbrella was deliberately left behind as an excuse to return and eavesdrop. Earthenware figures depict Paul Pry stooping because he liked looking through keyholes. The play became one of the great theatrical hits of its era and spawned Paul Pry memorabilia ranging from butter stamps to figures. Prints portraying Liston in this, his most celebrated role, inspired earthenware figures (fig. 51.1). Not shown here is a figure of Paul Pry impressed "SALT" with "Just Drop't in" painted on the base.[1]

Figure 51.1. *Mr. Liston as Paul Pry. "Well, if ever I do another kind action–may I be-"* Published by Ingrey & Madeley, London, circa 1825. © *Trustees of the British Museum.*

Figure 51.2. *PAUL PRY.* H: ~6". The figure wears striped pants associated with Paul Pry. Price A. *Andrew Dando Antiques.*

Figure 51.3. *PAUL PRY.* H: 6.1". Like the previous figure but with the umbrella positioned differently. Price A. *Andrew Dando Antiques.*

Figure 51.4. *PAUL PRY*, reverse of previous figure. *Andrew Dando Antiques.*

Figure 51.5. Paul Pry with his motto "I HOPE I DONT INTRUDE" on the base. Impressed "SALT". H: ~6". Price B.

Figure 51.6. *Paul Pry*. Impressed "SALT". H: 6.5". This figure is incorrectly titled as it portrays Lubin Log, another of Liston's famous character roles. Price A. *Woolley and Wallis Salisbury Salerooms Ltd.*

Figure 51.7. Paul Pry. H: 5.2". Price A.

Figure 51.8. Paul Pry. Attributed to "Sherratt." H: ~6.1". "Sherratt" made Paul Pry figures on different bases and in two sizes. This is the larger size. Price A.

Figure 51.9. Paul Pry, two figures on differently decorated bases. Attributed to "Sherratt." H: ~5.8" (L), 6.1" (R). The figure on the left has the more usual "Sherratt" base with two lines. The figures seem to be from the same molds, but firing shrinkage differed. Price A each.

Figure 51.10. Paul Pry. Attributed to "Sherratt." H: ~5.2". Significantly smaller than the previous "Sherratt" examples, and the base is from a different mold. Price A.

Figure 51.11. Paul Pry, two figures. Attributed to "Sherratt." H: ~5.2" (L), ~5.4" (R). On typical "Sherratt" bases. From different molds to previous "Sherratt" examples as the legs are fused. Size difference probably due to shrinkage in firing. Price A each.

Figure 51.12. Paul Pry, three figures. Attributed to "Sherratt." H: ~6.1" max. "Sherratt" made Paul Pry figures in two sizes, as shrinkage in firing alone cannot account for the significant differences in size. Price A each.

Figure 51.13. Paul Pry. Possibly made by Enoch Wood. H: ~6". Price A. *Andrew Dando Antiques.*

Figure 51.14. Paul Pry. Possibly made by Enoch Wood. H: ~6". The placement of the umbrella differs from that in the previous figure. Price A. *Andrew Dando Antiques.*

Figure 51.15. Paul Pry upon a goat, "I hope I dont intrude" on the base. Probably made at the Kirkaldy pot bank or by one of the other Scottish east coast potteries. H: 9.7". With predominantly under-glaze and possibly some enamel colors. Price C. *John Howard; www.antiquepottery.co.uk.*

52. Lubin Log

On November 20, 1812, John Liston appeared at Covent Garden as Lubin Log in the then-new play *Love, Law and Physic,* written by James Kenney. Lubin Log is a conceited and rather vulgar cockney who inherits a fortune and travels to York to marry a young lady. Alighting from the coach, mean-spirited Log takes his time giving the coach man a sixpenny tip, impressing on him that it is quite optional on his part, and the wording on some figures draws these words from the play.

Figure 52.1. *Mr. Liston in the Character of Lubin Log in Love, Law & Physic,* published 1826.

Figure 52.2. Lubin Log. Impressed "SALT". H. ~7". Price B.

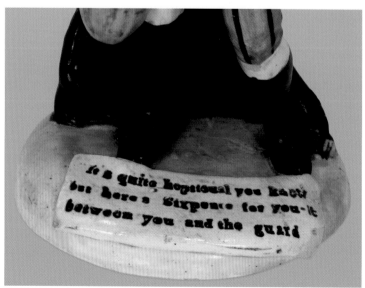

Figure 52.3. Lubin Log, base of previous figure. The words read "It s quite hoptional you know but here s sixpence for you. it between you and the guard".

68

Figure 52.4. Lubin Log. H: 7". Price A. *Collection of Arnold and Barbara Berlin.*

Figure 52.5. Lubin Log. Impressed "SALT". H: 6.5". Price A.

Figure 52.6. Lubin Log. H: ~6". Price A.

Figure 52.7. Lubin Log. Possibly made by Enoch Wood. H: 6.1". Price A. *Andrew Dando Antiques.*

Figure 52.8. Lubin Log. Possibly made by Enoch Wood. H: ~6.1". Price A. *Andrew Dando Antiques.*

Figure 52.9. Lubin Log (L) with Madame Vestris and Paul Pry. All possibly made by Enoch Wood. H: ~6.2" max. Price A each. *Andrew Dando Antiques.*

53. Sam Swipes

The stage role of Sam Swipes, a vulgar cockney, was a perfect fit for John Liston, the best-loved comic actor of his time. Liston was a hit as Sam Swipes in *Exchange no Robbery; or, The Diamond Ring*, which opened on August 12, 1820, at the Haymarket Theatre. The play was written by Theodore Hook, adapted from *He Would be a Soldier*, a play written in the eighteenth century. The tale is one of a young aristocrat who leaves his illegitimate child in the care of the landlord of an ale-house, sending regular funds for the boy's care. The boy flees his cruel presumed father, but, to the landlord's horror, the boy's natural father returns to claim him. Unable to produce the boy and afraid he will be charged with theft of the funds he has been receiving for years, the landlord substitutes his own son, Sam Swipes, as heir to the baronetcy. But elevated to a new role in society, young Sam Swipes is unable to abandon his plebeian ways.

The Enoch Wood figure model of Sam Swipes is after the Ingrey & Madeley print of January 1826 (fig. 53.1) or after the 1824 lithograph by J.W. Gear. The model was perhaps intended to stand with the theatrical portrayal of Liston as Van Dunder that this manufactory produced. The figure shown in figure 53.3 is sometimes interpreted as a butcher because the trousers are most frequently striped, but the resemblance to Sam Swipes is striking and the figure probably portrays him.

Figure 53.1. *Mr. Liston as Sam Swipes (in "Exchange no Robbery") No, am I a Gentleman! upon your soul tho' Mother?*, published by Ingrey & Madeley, January 1826. © *Trustees of the British Museum.*

Figure 53.2. Sam Swipes. Attributed to Enoch Wood. H: 6.4". The words on the front of the base are "No! am I a Gentleman? Upon your Soul tho' Mother." Impressed "20" beneath. This number has been noted on more than one example of this figure. Price B. *Andrew Dando Antiques.*

Figure 53.3. Sam Swipes. H: ~6". This figure model (sometimes interpreted as butcher because of the striped trousers) has also been recorded on a green square base. Price B. *John Howard; www. antiquepottery.co.uk.*

54. Van Dunder

On September 18, 1824, John Liston debuted at the Haymarket Theatre in the role of Van Dunder in John Poole's *'Twould Puzzle a Conjuror; or, the Two Peters.* Wearing baggy Dutch bloomers and silly shoes, Liston's character—his catch phrase was "'twould puzzle a conjuror"—was a bumbling Dutch burgomaster trying to figure out which of the numerous Pieters in the shipyard was Peter, Czar of Russia, working in disguise as a carpenter. The play was a revamp of Poole's earlier play, *The Burgomeister of Sardaam*, which had failed at Covent Garden in 1818. Figures of Van Dunder are derived from engravings of circa 1825.

Figure 54.1. *Mr. Liston as Van Dunder in 'Twould Puzzle a Conjuror "Read it indeed! that's very easily said read it!!"*, circa 1825.

Figure 54.2. Van Dunder. Made by Enoch Wood and impressed "WOOD". H: 7.1". The words from the play, "Read it indeed! that's very easily said, read it!!", are on the front of the base. The figure matches Enoch Wood figure fragments of circa 1828 excavated from St. Paul's Church, Burslem. Price B.

Figure 54.3. Base of previous figure of Van Dunder showing a blue painter's mark, a faintly impressed "K", and the impressed "WOOD" mark. Assorted impressed letters and numbers occur on many Wood figures, but this maker's mark is recorded on only two other figures, both of Van Dunder.

Figure 54.4. Van Dunder. Attributed to Enoch
Wood. H: 7.1". Price B. *Andrew Dando Antiques.*

Figure 54.5. Van Dunder. Probably made by Enoch
Wood. H: 7". Price A. *Collection of Arnold and
Barbara Berlin.*

Figure 54.6. Van Dunder. H: 7". Price B.
Andrew Dando Antiques.

Figure 54.7. Van Dunder, previous figure.
Andrew Dando Antiques.

55. Billy Waters and Douglas

Billy Waters, a former American slave who had lost his leg while serving in the British navy, was a familiar site in London's theatre district. In 1819, Lord Busby's *Costume of the Lower Orders of London* included a color lithograph of this peg-legged busker, known for his fiddle and lavishly cockaded hat. This illustration was probably the design source for the Staffordshire figures attributed to Enoch Wood (figs. 52.2–3). Enoch Wood figures of Billy Waters are larger than others, and they were routinely made without a dog. Today, crude Asian reproductions of this fine figure abound.

In November 1821, William Thomas Moncrieff's burletta *Tom and Jerry; or, Life in London*, an adaptation of Pierce Egan's *Life in London* published earlier that year, opened at the Adelphi Theatre. Although Billy Waters's presence in Egan's book was limited to a small illustration in a tavern scene, Moncrieff introduced the character of Billy Waters into his play. The play ran for over three hundred nights, breaking a sixty-two-night record held since 1728. Its success spawned multiple dramatizations of Egan's book that were performed on London and provincial stages. But the play caused Waters's demise. Those who could see him impersonated on the stage no longer felt obligated to support him on the street, and in March 1823, Billy died impoverished. His dying words were "Cuss him, dam Tommy Jerry." There was a voracious demand for images from *Life in London*, and varied simple engravings of the characters in the play adorned inexpensive street publications. A woodcut by the printer James Catnach shows Billy Waters accompanied by a dog. Smaller figures of Billy Waters routinely show Billy with a dog, and the need to paint Billy's skin black was sometimes overlooked.

The figure of Douglas, clad in a kilt, is sometimes paired with smaller figures of Billy Waters. *Douglas,* a play written by John Home, was first performed in 1756 and it remained popular for almost a century thereafter. The tragedy, based on a Scottish ballad, tells of Lady Randolph, who secretly mourns Lord Douglas, her husband by a prior clandestine marriage, and their baby that she had abandoned. In the play, Lady Randolph is reunited with her lost son, who claims his father's name.

In the manner of its time, *Douglas* was sometimes performed on stage on the same evening as *Life in London*, so audiences might see both plays for the same admission.[1] Only a potter's quirk or ignorance can account for Douglas's peg leg. Figures of Douglas are on the same scale as smaller figures of Billy Waters, and paired examples of these two figures occur.

Figure 55.1. *Billy Waters*, published by T. L. Busby, November 1819. *David Brass Rare Books, Inc.*

Figure 55.2. Billy Waters. Attributed to Enoch Wood. H: 8". Impressed "H" beneath. Fragments matching this figure were among Enoch Wood shards of circa 1825 excavated from the Burslem Old Town Hall site. Price C.

Figure 55.3. Billy Waters. Attributed to Enoch Wood. H: 8". All figures of Waters show his knee rather than his stump resting on his peg leg. Unlike smaller models, this figure never has a dog. Price C. *Andrew Dando Antiques.*

Figure 55.4. Billy Water. H: 6.7". Smaller than the previous model and includes a dog. Price B. *Brighton and Hove Museums.*

Figure 55.5. Billy Waters. H: 6.8". Price B. *The William Herbert and Nancy Hunt Collection.*

Figure 55.6. Billy Waters. H: 6.8". Unlike previous examples, the step is to the left of the figure. Billy's skin is not painted black. The dog is restored. Price A.

Figure 55.7. Billy Waters. H: 6.4". Pairs with the following figure of Douglas. Price B. *Brighton and Hove Museums.*

Figure 55.8. Douglas. H: 6.4". Pairs with the previous figure of Billy Waters. Note that Douglas has also been given a peg leg and both figures have dark skin. Price B. *Brighton and Hove Museums.*

Figure 55.9. *WATERS.* H: 6.5". Like many other examples of this size, the figure does not have black skin. Companion to the following *DOUGLAS.* Price C. *John Howard; www.antiquepottery.co.uk.*

Figure 55.10. *DOUGLAS*. H: 6.8". Companion to the previous *WATERS* and similarly titled. Price C. *The William Herbert and Nancy Hunt Collection.*

Figure 55.11. Douglas. H: 6.7". Douglas is rarer than Billy Waters. He is recognizable by his Scottish dress and bagpipes. Price B. *Collection of Arnold and Barbara Berlin.*

Figure 55.12. Douglas and Billy Waters, with spill vase. Attributed to "Sherratt." H: ~6". The base supports the attribution. Known only from this example. Price C.

56. African Sal

Pierce Egan's *Life in London* (1821) includes characters named African Sal and Bob, and one of George and Robert Cruikshank's engravings for the book shows them dancing a *pas de deux*. In 1821, *Tom and Jerry; or, Life in London*, a stage adaptation of *Life in London*, transformed these two characters into African Sal and Dusty Bob, and their dance became one of the play's highlights. Cruikshank's representation of the dance was mimicked in engravings and cheap wood cuts, with African Sal looking as she does in the earthenware figure. Mr. Walbourn in the role of Dusty Bob was so popular that Cruickshank sold engravings of him at the Adelphi Theatre, but no figures of Dusty Bob are known. Only one pre-Victorian earthenware figure of African Sal is recorded. Fragments of a figure matching African Sal and the base of a figure titled *Dusty Bob* are among the Enoch Wood shards excavated from the Burslem Old Town Hall site.

Figure 56.1. Detail of *Lowest Life in London. Tom, Jerry and Logic among the unsophisticated Sons and Daughters of Nature at All Max in the East*, by George and Robert Cruikshank, 1821.

Figure 56.3. African Sal, made of porcelaneous material rather than earthenware. H: 4.2". Derby also made a similar figure in porcelain. *Richard Montgomery.*

Figure 56.2. *AFRICAN SAL*. Attributed to Enoch Wood. H: 3.8". Known from only this figure. Matches a figure fragment from the Burslem Old Town Hall site. Price C. *Brighton and Hove Museums.*

57. Robinson Crusoe

Robinson Crusoe by Daniel Defoe, published in 1719, is one of the earliest novels. In this fictional autobiography, Crusoe spends twenty-eight years as a castaway on a tropical island. The book was first dramatized on the English stage in the eighteenth century. The figure of Robinson Crusoe is the earliest form of a Staffordshire figure that was to be popular in the Victorian era. Crusoe wears the distinctive garb and signature hat that he wore in the frontispiece print of the 1719 edition of the book, and these were to be associated with him thereafter.

Figure 57.1. Engraving of Robinson Crusoe for the frontispiece of *Robinson Crusoe*, published 1719.

Figure 57.2. Robinson Crusoe. H: 6.2". Price A. *Andrew Dando Antiques.*

58. Dick Turpin

Dick Turpin (1705–1739) was, in today's parlance, a gangster. His crimes included cattle rustling, highway robbery, and murder. *The Life of Richard Turpin,* published in 1739, the year Turpin was hanged, turned this rogue into a legend. William Harrison Ainsworth's romantic novel *Rookwood* (1834) established Turpin on his horse, Black Bess, as a daring hero, and Turpin was to be popular in ballads and on the stage for much of the rest of the century. The transitional figure shown here dates from circa 1835. A pair of equestrian figures of the same period portraying Dick Turpin and Tom King (Turpin's associate in crime) is recorded. Turpin appears as in the figure shown below, and King is similarly styled to the pair.[1]

Figure 58.1. Dick Turpin. H: 8.7". Price B. *Bonhams.*

59. Jack Sheppard

A figure titled *SHEPPARD*, known from one example, portrays Jack Sheppard (1702–1724), a colorful criminal who rose to fame in London in the early eighteenth century. In 1723, young Jack, a model carpenter's apprentice, turned to crime. After four imprisonments and escapes, each executed with daring bravado, Jack was arrested for the final time. This time, he was weighed down with three hundred pounds of weights and kept under round-the-clock observation. By now, Jack was immensely popular with the poorer classes, and his importance was such that the king's painter, James Thornhill, visited to paint his portrait. But on November 11, 1724, Jack Sheppard was hanged. Two hundred thousand people turned out to give their hero a celebratory send-off.

Jack Sheppard lived on in the hearts of the public as a folk hero, and ballads and pantomimes that appeared shortly after his death romanticized him. His character inspired Macheath in John Gay's *The Beggars' Opera* (1728). *The Threepenny Opera* (a twentieth-century updating of *The Beggars' Opera*) included the song *Mack the Knife*, which became a twentieth-century hit.

A melodrama by W.T. Moncrieff titled *Jack Sheppard, The Housebreaker, or London in 1724* was published in 1825. Performances of this play must have inspired the figure of Jack Sheppard. The most obvious nineteenth-century reincarnation of Sheppard was in the novel *Jack Sheppard* by William Harrison Ainsworth, published in 1839, but the figure shown here predates that publication.

Figure 59.1. *SHEPPARD*. Possibly attributable to the Box Title Group. H: 10.8". Known from only this example. Price B.

79

60. Unidentified Theatrical Figures

A late eighteenth-century figure of a lady in classical garb, with one arm raised as if sleepwalking, is known from one example and is not shown here. It has been suggested that it portrays Sarah Siddons as Lady Macbeth.[1]

Figure 60.1. Twin brothers dueling, the one run through with a sword, with two classically attired children, with bocage. H: 9". A puzzling subject that probably portrays a theatrical scene of its day. Price B.

Figure 60.2. Theatrically attired couple, two examples. H: ~7". The group on the left (his head is restored) is a transitional figure from the 1830s probably portraying a theatrical scene. The group on the right is a later Victorian example of the same subject. Price A each.

Figure 60.3. Theatrically posed gentleman in plaid garb. H: 7.5". Known only from this example and another in the Brighton and Hove Museums. Price B. *The William Herbert and Nancy Hunt Collection.*

Figure 60.4. Theatrically posed gentleman in plaid garb, reverse of previous figure. *The William Herbert and Nancy Hunt Collection.*

Figure 60.5. Theatrical character. H: ~5". At the back, the figure is flat and a small container at the base serves as a spill holder. Two other figures (one female, one male) formed in the same manner have been noted, and all are thought to represent theatrical characters. Price A. *John Howard; www.antiquepottery.co.uk.*

Patriotic Themes
61. Britannia

Britannia has personified Britain since Roman times; the lion beside her symbolizes England. The image of Britannia was common in engravings, and one no doubt inspired her replication in clay. Only two models of Britannia are known. The larger model (figs. 61.2–4) was made by Enoch Wood/ Wood & Caldwell. It occurs more frequently than the smaller model and is often decorated with silver luster, indicating manufacture from 1805, the year in which silver lustering was introduced commercially. The smaller model (figs. 61.5–6) is known only from the examples shown.

Figure 61.1. *BRITANNIA Crowning the DUKE of WELLINGTON with VICTORY after the ever Memorable Battle of WATERLOO fought on the 16 17 & 18 June 1815 against the French Army commanded by BUONAPARTE in person,* published by W. B. Walker, London. *Martyn Edgell Antiques Ltd.*

Figure 61.2. Britannia. Impressed "WOOD & CALDWELL" and incised "Burslem". H: 9.3". Made between 1805 (when silver lustering was introduced) and 1818 (when the Wood & Caldwell partnership dissolved). Price C.

Figure 61.5. *BRITANNIA*, with bocage. H: ~7". Price C. *The Moore Collection.*

Figure 61.3. Britannia. Impressed "WOOD & CALDWELL". H: 9.2". Typical Wood & Caldwell flowers are on the base. Price C. *Brighton and Hove Museums.*

Figure 61.4. Britannia, reverse of the previous figure. The mark is impressed toward the bottom. *Brighton and Hove Museums.*

Figure 61.6. Britannia, with bocage. H: ~7". Price B.

62. Saint George and the Dragon

There are no historical sources for the existence of Saint George; rather his origins are hagiographical. By the second millennium, Saint George was well established in European culture, and he was to become a recurrent figure in the iconography of many nations. Jacobus de Voragine's popular medieval book of hagiographies, written between 1260 and 1275, tells the story of Saint George and the dragon. A beautiful princess was to be sacrificed to an evil dragon, but Saint George, after making the sign of the cross, slayed the dragon with his lance—and it is in this pose that Saint George is traditionally shown. By those times, the dragon embodied the evil that Christian Crusaders believed they were fighting. Crusaders revered Saint George and adopted his red and white cross as their own. From the thirteenth century, he was gradually accepted as the patron saint of England; his cross was adopted as England's flag and it remains so today, although other entities too claim Saint George and his flag as their own.

The theme of Saint George and the dragon has been represented in art for centuries. A print or one of the bronze statuettes of this or a similar equestrian subject by the sculptor Francesco Fanelli (circa 1577–1661) probably inspired the earthenware figures. A November 1783 invoice from Ralph Wood to Josiah Wedgwood indicates that such figures were being made at that early date. Frank Falkner in *The Wood Family of Burslem* notes that Ralph Wood made this figure impressed "23" in both colored glazes and enamels.

Figure 62.1. *St. George on Horseback Fighting with the Dragon*, after Raphael, circa 1627. ©*Victoria and Albert Museum, London.*

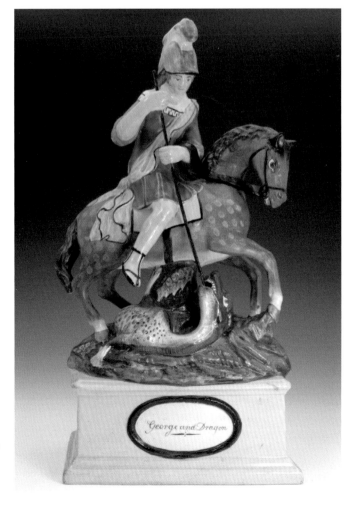

Figure 62.2. *George and Dragon.* H: 14.2". Figures of Hudibras and the Vicar and Moses stand on bases formed and titled in the same manner. Price C. *John Howard; www.antiquepottery.co.uk.*

Figure 62.3. *George & Dragon*. H: 14.2". Like the previous example but titled differently. Price C. *Collection of Arnold and Barbara Berlin.*

Figure 62.4. St. George and the dragon. Attributed to Wood & Caldwell. Poorly incised "Burslem". H: 11" (excluding spear), L: 9". Made between 1805 (when silver lustering was introduced) and 1818 (when the Wood & Caldwell partnership dissolved). Larger than the following example from the same pot bank. Price C.

Figure 62.5. St. George and the dragon. Impressed "WOOD & CALDWELL". Incised "Burslem". H: 8" (excluding spear), L: 6.8". Significantly smaller than the previous example. Wood & Caldwell made this subject in two sizes, with notable differences in the form of both St. George and his horse. Price B. *Collection of Michael J, Smith.*

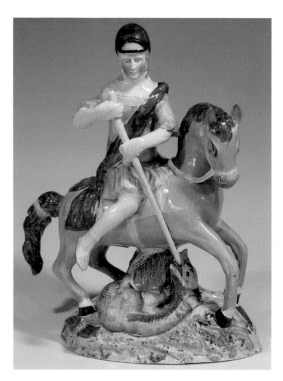

Figure 62.6. St. George and the dragon. H: ~11". Price B. *John Howard; www.antiquepottery.co.uk.*

Figure 62.7. St. George and the dragon. H: ~11". Price B.

Figure 62.7. *SAINT GEORGE & DRAGON*. Attributed to "Sherratt." H: 11". A rare figure known from only this example. Price D. *The Earle Collection, #631.*

63. Royal Arms

The royal coat of arms of the United Kingdom is portrayed on earthenware spill vases. These are uncommon and desirable. In the center of each vase is the shield on the coat of arms, depicting England's three lions passant, a Scottish lion rampant, and an Irish harp. The French phrase *"Honi soit qui mal y pense"* on a garter surrounding the shield is the motto of the Order of the Garter, the supreme order of chivalry founded by King Edward III in 1348. At the base of the shield are national floral emblems—a rose, thistle, and shamrock—and the French phrase *"Dieu et Mon Droit"* (God and My Right) that King Richard I is thought to have used as a password at the Battle of Gisor in 1198. In the fifteenth century, King Henry VI selected these words as the royal motto.

Smaller lion and unicorn figure pairs portray the English lion and Scottish unicorn that are the supporters on the royal coat of arms. The unicorn is chained because in medieval times a unicorn was believed to be a dangerous beast that only a virgin could tame.

Figure 63.1. Royal armorial spill vase. H: 7.5", L: 8.7". A particularly rare spill vase. Price E.

Figure 63.2. Reverse of previous spill vase.

Figure 63.3. Royal armorial spill vase. Impressed "WALTON". H: 5.7". Although well known, this group is uncommon. A similar example in the Fitzwilliam Museum is on a pale marbled base. Price D.

Figure 63.4. Royal supporters spill vase, with sheep. Attributed to "Sherratt." H: 8.8". Like the following "Sherratt" spill vases, this is rare. The swag of leaves and berries on the neck of the vase also occurs on the apron swags of "Sherratt" marbled table bases. Price E.

Figure 63.5. Royal supporters spill vase. Attributed to "Sherratt." H: ~9". Like the previous example but on a different typical "Sherratt" base. Price C. *The Moore Collection.*

Figure 63.6. Royal supporters spill vase. Attributed to "Sherratt." H: 8.3". The small flowers to either side of the base of the vase are typical of "Sherratt" but are normally found on bocages. Price D. *The William Herbert and Nancy Hunt Collection.*

Figure 63.7. Royal supporters with man, woman, dog, and squirrels. H: 6.4". A curiously confused concoction of the royal supporters and an array of figures that should be placed in other groups. Price C. *Brighton and Hove Museums.*

Figure 63.8. Royal supporters, reverse of previous example. The mélange of characters on this group includes a man normally found with performing animal troupes and a woman usually found reading. Loss to what was possibly a bocage has occurred. *Brighton and Hove Museums.*

Figure 63.9. Royal supporters, a lion and a unicorn, a pair, with bocages. Impressed "WALTON". H: 6.1" (L), 5.9" (R). The lion can occur with or without a ball beneath his paw. Price D. *Image courtesy of The Potteries Museum & Art Gallery, Stoke-on-Trent, UK.*

Figure 63.10. Royal supporter lion, with bocage. Impressed "WALTON". H: ~6". Like the lion in the previous pair but made without a ball beneath his paw. Price B.

Figure 63.11. Royal supporter lion, with bocage. Impressed "WALTON". H: ~6". Like the previous lion but with different bocage flowers. Price B. *Collection of Michael J. Smith.*

Figure 63.12. Royal supporters, a lion and a unicorn, a pair, with bocages. H: ~6".
These spectacular bocage leaves occur on a few other Walton-style figures that lack features supporting an attribution. Price D.

Figure 63.13. Detail of the bocage on the lion in the previous pair.

Figure 63.14. Royal supporters, a lion and a unicorn, a pair.
H: ~3.5". Price B.

Figure 63.15. Royal supporter lion.
H: ~3.5". Price Á.

Important People
64. King William III

Confusion arises over a striking figure of an equestrian attired in Roman garb. The figure is sometimes described as King William III, sometimes as the Duke of Cumberland. The confusion may arise because the Duke of Cumberland's name was William. In 1770, an equestrian statue of William, Duke of Cumberland was placed in Cavendish Square, London. The statue was removed in 1868, and there is no record of its appearance. More likely, the equestrian figure represents King William III, the Dutch Protestant that Parliament placed on the throne in 1689. King William's victory at the Battle of the Boyne in 1690 secured a Protestant succession for the British monarchy. Equestrian statues of King William III popped up across England in the eighteenth and nineteenth centuries, and the king resembles Julius Caesar in all the statues. The reason for the resemblance is that medals struck to commemorate King William's military victory at the siege of Namur in 1695 portray him on horseback in Roman dress, a commander's baton in his right hand. This flattering "Caesar theme" was then adopted for statues and, in turn, for figures.

Figure 64.1 Pearlware plate commemorating King William III, circa 1800. Diameter: 6.2". The transfer print shows William as he appears in figural form. *Martyn Edgell Antiques Ltd.*

Figure 64.2. King William III. Possibly made by Enoch Wood/Wood & Caldwell. H: 15.7". Price C. *Collection of Arnold and Barbara Berlin.*

Figure 64.3. King William III. Probably made by Ralph Wood. H: 15.5". The support under the horse's belly in the previous example is now beneath the chest and forelegs. The delicate marbling and the rainbow palette on the support is typical of Ralph Wood figures. Price C. *Northeast Auctions.*

Figure 64.4. King William III. Possibly made by Ralph Wood. H: 15.5". The horse is supported beneath the chest and forelegs, as in the previous example. Price C. © *Victoria and Albert Museum, London.*

Figure 64.5. King William III. H: ~8". Price C.

65. King George IV

King George IV reigned from 1820 to 1830. The figure shown, known from only this example, strongly resembles his many portraits.

Figure 65.1. Engraving of King George IV, after Robert Bowyer, 1827.

Figure 65.2. King George IV. H: 6.1".
Price D. *Brighton and Hove Museums.*

66. Queen Victoria

Queen Victoria ascended the throne in June 1837. This figure of the young queen is known from only one example. It is adapted from the figure of the celebrated diva Maria Malibran, who died in 1836 (fig. 49.2). When Miss Malibran died, the figure of her was recycled to portray Queen Victoria by changing the title and placing a crown alongside. That the crown is not upon Victoria's head suggests that the figure predates her coronation on June 28, 1838.

Figure 66.1. *HER MAJESTY QUEEN VICTORIA.* Attributed to "Sherratt." H: 10.5". Known from only this example. This is the latest datable table-base figure. Price E. *Jonathan Horne.*

67. Duke of Clarence or Duke of York

The figure shown is incised "Stephan F", this probably being the mark of Pierre Stephan, the famed free-lance modeler best remembered for his work for Derby. Only two earthenware figures are recorded marked thus (see also fig. 76.1). Between about 1794 and 1798, Stephan modeled figures of admirals for Derby, and this earthenware figure, in much the same style, was possibly also modeled in that period.[1]

The figure has strong Hanoverian facial features and may represent Prince William, Duke of Clarence (1765–1837), who was crowned King William IV in 1830. His portrait by Sir Martin Archer Shee hanging in the National Portrait Gallery shows the Duke of Clarence standing before a flag and cannon. The Duke served in New York at the tail end of the American War of Independence (1775–1783). The flag behind the earthenware figure is intended to be the first American flag, called the Grand Union flag, which had thirteen red and white stripes.

A figure very like the earthenware figure occurs in Derby porcelain. The facial features appear to be slightly different, and the flag bears the crosses of the saints Andrew and George. This figure (unmarked but incised "391") is thought to represent Prince Frederick Augustus, Duke of York (1763–1827).[2] The Duke of York (brother to the Duke of Clarence) had a distinguished military career. Although he never served in America, it is possible that the earthenware figure portrays him.

Figure 67.1. The Duke of Clarence or the Duke of York. H: 11.5". Price E. *Andrew Dando Antiques.*

Figure 67.2. "Stephan F", thought to be the mark of the modeler Pierre Stephan, is incised on the back of this figure.

68. Oliver Cromwell

In the seventeenth century, Oliver Cromwell (1599–1658) helped overthrow England's monarchy, and he became Lord Protector of the new republican commonwealth. Cromwell seems an unlikely subject for a later earthenware figure, but the figure is after an engraving from George Frederick Raymond's *A New, Universal and Impartial History of England* that was published in serial form in the late 1780s.

Figure 68.1. *Oliver Cromwell*, after Samuel Wale, circa 1790.

Figure 68.2. *O. Cromwell*. Attributed to Ralph Wood. H: 9.1".
An example of this figure impressed "20" is recorded.[1] Price C.
Brighton and Hove Museums.

69. John Wilkes

John Wilkes (circa 1726–1797) was a great libertarian, and today he is considered the founding father of British radicalism, the movement that came to advocate improved parliamentary representation. Despite his notoriously dissolute lifestyle, Wilkes was enormously popular with the populace. His pursuit of liberty also fueled the American revolutionary struggle and ultimately influenced the freedoms that Britons and Americans now enjoy. These are the only known pre-Victorian figure of Wilkes. He holds a scroll inscribed "The Rights of the People."

Figure 69.1. *John Wilkes Esqr.,* after Robert Edge Pine, 1768.

Figure 69.2. John Wilkes. H: 10". He holds a scroll inscribed "The Rights of the People." Price C. *Brighton and Hove Museums.*

Figure 69.3. John Wilkes. H: 8.5". He holds a scroll inscribed "The Rights of the People." Price C. *The William Herbert and Nancy Hunt Collection.*

70. Benjamin Franklin

Benjamin Franklin (1706–1790) was one of America's Founding Fathers and a leading statesman, author, publisher, and inventor. As a scientist, he is best remembered for his work with electricity. The figure's source is not known. Statues in America showing Franklin posed in the same manner are of a later date. Possibly this pose suggests Franklin drawing electricity from the sky. The medal around Franklin's neck may be the Royal Society of London's Copley Medal, which was awarded him in 1753 "on account of his curious Experiments and Observations on Electricity."

Figure 70.2. Dr. Franklin. Attributed to Ralph Wood; impressed "43". H: 13". Price D. *The William Herbert and Nancy Hunt Collection.*

Figure 70.1. *Dr. Franklin.* Attributed to Ralph Wood; impressed "42". "Electricity" is painted on the open book he holds. H: 13.4". Price D. *Wisbech & Fenland Museum.*

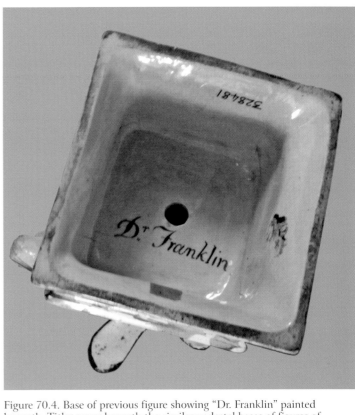

Figure 70.4. Base of previous figure showing "Dr. Franklin" painted beneath. Titles occur beneath the similar pedestal bases of figures of St. John, St. Peter, and Jupiter. *Brighton and Hove Museums.*

Figure 70.3. *Dr. Franklin* (title painted beneath the base). Probably made by Ralph Wood or Enoch Wood/Wood & Caldwell. H: 13.2". Ralph Wood used this pedestal base with paterae for some figures. Price C. *Brighton and Hove Museums.*

Figure 70.5. *Franklin.* Benjamin Franklin. Attributed to Ralph Wood. H: 11". Titling of this form is typical of Ralph Wood figures decorated in a harsher palette. Price C. © *Christie's Images Limited 2014.*

71. Isaac Newton

Isaac Newton (1642–1727) is the most acclaimed mathematician and scientist in the history of mankind. Figures of Newton stand alongside a celestial globe, and the "1680" painted beneath the globe refers to Newton's comet of 1680. The model is probably after a reduced-scale eighteenth-century plaster. An example at Temple Newsam House (16.199/47) stands on a square base painted with only a line, and it is impressed "LEEDS POTTERY".

Figure 71.2. *Newton*. Attributed to Ralph Wood. H: 12". Price B. © *Victoria and Albert Museum, London.*

Figure 71.1. Isaac Newton. Impressed "Ra. Wood Burslem" and "137" on the reverse of the base. H: 12.5". Price B. *Brighton and Hove Museums.*

72. John Milton

John Milton (1608–1674) is best known for his poem *Paradise Lost*, and a scene from *Paradise Lost* is on the column beside each figure of Milton. In the eighteenth century, Derby made a figure of Milton to pair with a figure of Shakespeare. The Derby figure is posed in the same manner as the earthenware figure and may have influenced in its modeling. However, it is more likely that the earthenware figure is after a plaster. A plaster by John Cheere dated 1749 has been recorded,[1] and the initials of the plaster maker Peter Vanina, "P. V.", occur on some earthenware figures.[2] Falkner notes a bronze-glazed example of this figure marked "WOOD & CALDWELL".

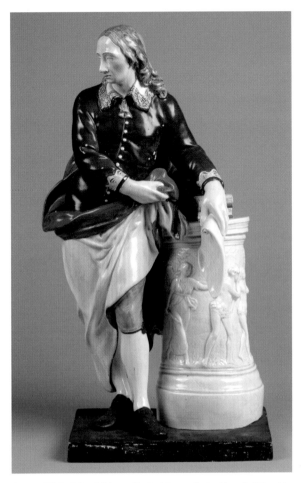

Figure 72.2. John Milton. Probably made by Enoch Wood/ Wood & Caldwell. H: 18.7". Price B. © *Victoria and Albert Museum, London.*

Figure 72.1. John Milton. H: 15.5". Pairs with a figure of Shakespeare (fig. 74.5). Price B. *Image courtesy of The Potteries Museum & Art Gallery, Stoke-on-Trent, UK.*

Figure 72.3. John Milton. H: 10.8". Price B. *Brighton and Hove Museums.*

Figure 72.4. John Milton, reverse of previous figure.

73. Geoffrey Chaucer

Geoffrey Chaucer (circa 1343–1400) is known as the father of English literature. The design source for earthenware figures of Chaucer is not known.

Figure 73.1. *Chaucer*. Attributed to Ralph Wood; impressed "155". H: 12". Price B. *Andrew Dando Antiques.*

Figure 73.2. Chaucer. Attributed to Ralph Wood; impressed "137". Price B.

Figure 73.3. *Chaucer*. Attributed to Ralph Wood. H: 12.4". Titling is in the small, red script routinely found on Ralph Wood figures. Price B. © *Victoria and Albert Museum, London.*

Figure 73.5. Chaucer. Probably made by Ralph Wood. H: ~12". Price B. *Andrew Dando Antiques.*

Figure 73.4. Chaucer. Probably made by Ralph Wood. H: 12.5". Made with a hole in the back of the base. Price B. *Image courtesy of The Potteries Museum & Art Gallery, Stoke-on-Trent, UK.*

Figure 73.6. Chaucer. Made by Ralph Wood; impressed "W". H: 12.6". The back of the base is unpainted, and "W" is impressed on it. Price A. *Brettells Auctioneers.*

74. William Shakespeare

William Shakespeare (1564–1616) is England's best known bard. Figures of Shakespeare are based upon Shakespeare's monument in Westminster Abbey. The monument was designed by William Kent and executed by Peter Scheemakers. Large figures of Shakespeare on low, rectangular bases can be decorated very lavishly, and they are traditionally attributed to Enoch Wood/Wood & Caldwell. Enoch Wood hid earthenware as a time capsule for later discovery, and a large figure of Shakespeare was unearthed behind a wall he had erected in 1810.[1] Some of these large figures have "P. V." incised into the base, suggesting that they were derived from reduced scale plaster figures produced by Peter Vanina. A smaller figure of Shakespeare (fig. 74.6) is after a Derby model of circa 1758, which is also after Shakespeare's statue in Westminster Abbey.

All figures of Shakespeare have a scroll at the bard's side. Sometimes words from *The Tempest*, Act 4, Scene 1, are on the scroll, and the words may be slightly modified from the wording on the Westminster Abbey statue. More often, scribble (to simulate words) is present. As on the Westminster Abbey statue, the mask of Tragedy is visible on the front of the pedestal beside Shakespeare, and the heads of Queen Elizabeth I, Richard III, and Henry V are at the base of the pedestal.

Figure 74.1. William Shakespeare. Probably made by Enoch Wood/Wood & Caldwell. H: 18". Note the exquisite gilding on the clothing and the gilded words on the scroll. Price C. *Andrew Dando Antiques.*

Figure 74.2. William Shakespeare, detail of the scroll on the previous figure. *Andrew Dando Antiques.*

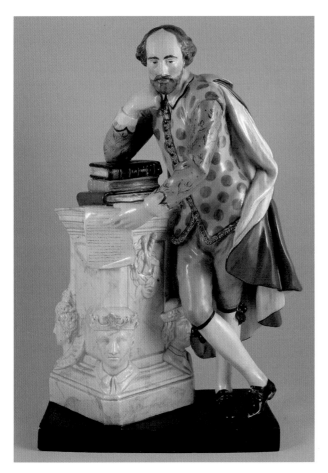

Figure 74.3. William Shakespeare. Probably made by Enoch Wood/Wood & Caldwell. H: 18". Incised "P. V.", probably the initials of Peter Vanina who may have supplied a plaster mold for this figure. Scribble rather than script is on the scroll. Price C. *Andrew Dando Antiques.*

Figure 74.4. William Shakespeare. Probably made by Enoch Wood/Wood & Caldwell. The gilding is lavish. H: 18.2". Price B. *Collection of Arnold and Barbara Berlin.*

Figure 74.5. William Shakespeare. H: 15.7". Pairs with a figure of Milton (fig. 72.1). Price B. *Image courtesy of The Potteries Museum & Art Gallery, Stoke-on-Trent, UK.*

Figure 74.6. *SHAKESPEAR* (on the scroll). William Shakespeare. H: ~11". Smaller than the previous figures of Shakespeare and known from only this example. After the Derby model of circa 1758. Words from *The Tempest* are on the scroll. Price C. *Collection of Barbara W. Kummel.*

75. Anthony van Dyck and Peter Paul Rubens

Figures of the two Flemish Baroque painters Anthony van Dyck (1599–1641) and Peter Paul Rubens (1577–1640) are after mid-eighteenth century Bow porcelain models, which are in turn after John Michael Rysbrack.

Figure 75.1. Anthony van Dyck. Possibly made by Enoch Wood/Wood & Caldwell. H: 22.2". Price C. *Dallas Auction Gallery.*

Figure 75.2. Peter Paul Rubens (L) and Anthony van Dyck (R). Possibly made by Enoch Wood/Wood & Caldwell. H: 22.2". The figures' heads, torsos, and legs are molded identically. Price C each. © *Christie's Images Limited 2014.*

76. Duke of Wellington

The identity of the figure shown here is frequently a topic of speculation, but an example in the Potteries Museum is titled *Duke Wellington* (fig. 76.10), so perhaps all examples represent that military hero. Arthur Wellesley, 1st Duke of Wellington (1769–1852), was a leading military figure of his era. He is best remembered for commanding the allied forces that defeated Napoleon at the Battle of Waterloo in 1815. Wellington served as prime minister from 1828 to 1830 and again in 1834. Until his death, he remained commander-in-chief of the army.

The figure was originally modeled by Pierre Stephan, and one example with his mark incised in the body is shown. It is not known whether Stephan was still active at the time that Wellington rose to fame, and Stephan could have made the original model several years earlier to portray some other individual. Later, the model may have been adapted to sometimes include a garter star on the chest and cannon balls at the feet, and it perhaps then came to be identified with the Duke of Wellington.

Figure 76.1. Duke of Wellington. H: 12.4". "Stephan F," the mark of the modeler Pierre Stephan, is incised on the back of this figure. The rim of the canon is particularly thick and is impressed "BUONAPARTE". Note the gilding. A sword is lost from his hand. Price C. *Angus Northeast.*

Figure 76.2. "Stephan *f.*" *(fecit)*, thought to be the mark of the modeler Pierre Stephan, incised on the back of the previous figure. The same mark is on another military figure (fig. 67.1). *Angus Northeast.*

Figure 76.3. Duke of Wellington. H: ~12.4". Like the previous figure but unmarked and less lavishly decorated. Also, the plume atop the hat is present. Price B. *John Howard; www. antiquepottery.co.uk.*

Figure 76.4. Duke of Wellington. H: 12". Like previous figures, but cannon balls and a garter star on his chest have been added. Price C.

Figure 76.5. Duke of Wellington, previous figure showing the scabbard decorated with silver luster.

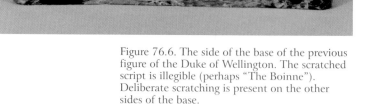

Figure 76.6. The side of the base of the previous figure of the Duke of Wellington. The scratched script is illegible (perhaps "The Boinne"). Deliberate scratching is present on the other sides of the base.

Figure 76.7. Duke of Wellington. H: 13". Like the previous figure. Price C. © *Victoria and Albert Museum, London.*

Figure 76.8. Duke of Wellington. H: 12". Without a garter star, scabbard, and cannon balls. The base is decorated with pink luster. Price C. *Nick Burton.*

Figure 76.9. Duke of Wellington. H: 11.4". Note the tassels on the sides of the hat, also recorded on other examples with similar colorful bases. Without the scabbard, garter star, and cannon balls on some previous examples. Price C.

Figure 76.10. *Duke Wellington.* H: 11.5". The only titled example recorded. Made without the scabbard, cannon balls, and garter star. Note the small lions on the pink luster base. The restored cannon is wood. Price B. *Image courtesy of The Potteries Museum & Art Gallery, Stoke-on-Trent, UK.*

Figure 76.11. Duke of Wellington. H: 12.7". Similar to the previous three figures, but slight differences suggest different molds were used. Price B. *Elinor Penna.*

77. Horatio Nelson and Napoleon Bonaparte

Horatio Nelson, 1st Viscount Nelson, (1758–1805) was the much-acclaimed hero whose victories at sea and death in battle secured his status as a beloved hero. Nelson is commemorated in numerous monuments and artworks, but only one example of this earthenware figure is recorded. Stylistically, the figure resembles other figures modeled by Pierre Stephan, and it may also be Stephan's design.

Napoleon Bonaparte (1769–1821) rose from humble beginnings to become one of the greatest military commanders of all time and the first Emperor of France. From the final years of the eighteenth century until his defeat at the Battle of Waterloo in 1815, he dominated the world stage with successive campaigns aimed at ensuring French dominance. He abdicated in 1815 and died in exile on the island of St. Helena.

Figure 77.1. Horatio Nelson. H: 11.6". Price D. *Bonhams*.

Figure 77.2. Napoleon Bonaparte. H: 20.5". Price C. *The William Herbert and Nancy Hunt Collection.*

78. Cornelius van Tromp

Cornelius van Tromp (1629–1691) was the Dutch admiral renowned for his naval contests against England's Admiral Blake. Van Tromp visited England in 1675, and King Charles II granted him a baronetcy. John Wood's ledger of 1785 records this figure subject decorated in both enamels and colored glazes.

Figure 78.1. *Cornelis Tromp*, by Sir Peter Lely, circa 1675.

Figure 78.2. *Van Tromp*. Attributed to Ralph Wood; impressed "38". H: 10.4". Price B. *Image courtesy of The Potteries Museum & Art Gallery, Stoke-on-Trent, UK.*

Figure 78.3. *Van Tromp*, reverse of previous figure with "38" impressed on the undecorated back of the plinth. *Image courtesy of The Potteries Museum & Art Gallery, Stoke-on-Trent, UK.*

Figure 78.4. *Van Tromp.*
Attributed to Ralph
Wood; impressed "37".
H: ~10.4". With losses.
Price A. *Elinor Penna.*

Figure 78.5. Cornelius van Tromp.
H: ~9". Price B. *Andrew
Dando Antiques.*

110

79. Sailors and Soldiers

Britain's late eighteenth and early nineteenth century military and naval battles spanned the globe. Sailors and soldiers served in far-flung places for long periods of time, and a figure was a memento of a loved one. In 1744, Boitard's engraving of the *Sailor's Farewell* and *Sailor's Return* were printed with sentimental ballads, and paintings, prints, and caricatures echoed this refrain through the war-torn early 1800s. Possibly a print—or merely the theme itself—inspired earthenware groups portraying such scenes. The groups frequently occur paired, but examples with good bocages are difficult to procure. The departing sailor usually has a bundle of possessions at his feet, while the returning sailor clutches a money bag. Other figures of sailors are identifiable by the sailor's distinctive attire that includes striped trousers, neckerchiefs, and characteristic caps or hats. Some sailors stand beside an anchor or clutch a bag of coins in one hand. Figures of sailors' lasses sometimes occur to pair with figures of sailors.

Figures of soldiers are quite uncommon and most portray Loyal Volunteers, the men who volunteered to defend Britain from the threat of invasion posed by revolutionary France. In 1794, Parliament issued a call to arms, and by 1804 volunteer forces had peaked at over 380,000. The men were issued uniforms that might include a white cross-belt (as seen routinely on figures) denoting the ability to fire a musket. Thomas Rowlandson's aquatints of soldiers (1798–1799) show soldiers in drill positions, and these probably influenced the design of similarly posed figures. Figures of peg-legged soldiers also occur, as maimed soldiers must have been an unremarkable sight in that day.

Figure 79.1. *The Sailor's Return,* published by Robert Sayer, 1793.

Figure 79.2. *FAREWELL, RETURN.* A sailor and his lass, a pair of groups, with bocages. H: 9.2". *"DOLLORS"* is on the chest at the sailor's feet. Price C. *Andrew Dando Antiques.*

Figure 79.3. *SAILoRe Return*. A sailor and his lass, with bocage. H: 8.7". Price B. *Image courtesy of The Potteries Museum & Art Gallery, Stoke-on-Trent, UK.*

Figure 79.4. Sailor's return. Sailor and his lass, with bocage. H: 9". The sailor clutches his money bag as he gazes adoringly at his lass. Perhaps from the same pot bank as the previous example. Price B.

Figure 79.5. Sailor's return and departure. Sailor and his lass, a pair of groups, with bocages. H: 9.3" (L), 9.5" (R). Price B. *Brighton and Hove Museums.*

Figure 79.6. *Departure, Return*. Sailor and his lass, a pair of groups, with bocages. H: 9" (L), 8.6" (R). Price B. *Collection of Michael J. Smith.*

Figure 79.7. Sailor's return. Sailor and his lass, with bocage. Attributed to Patriotic Group. H: 9.2". Unlike previous examples, the lass stands to greet her sailor. The base, bocage, and painting style support the attribution. Price B. *Brighton and Hove Museums.*

Figure 79.8. Sailor's return. A sailor and his lass, with bocage. Attributed to Patriotic Group. H: ~9.2". Possible restored clasped hands; money bag lost. The floral sprigs on the base are specific to the Patriotic Group. A Farewell group on the same base is in the National Maritime Museum (AAA6058). Price B.

Figure 79.9. Sailor, wife, and child, a pair. H: ~9.8". Made without bocages. Price B. *John Howard; www.antiquepottery.co.uk.*

Figure 79.10. Sailor, wife, and child, a pair. H: 9.8" (L), 9.6" (R). Made without bocages. Price B. *Brighton and Hove Museums.*

Figure 79.11. Sailor's wife and child, with bocage. H: 9.2". Price B.

Figure 79.12. Sailor's wife and child, with bocage. H: 9". Price A. *Marcia Stancil Antiques, Wilson, North Carolina.*

Figure 79.13. Sailor. H: ~5.4". Price A.

Figure 79.14. Sailor. H: 5". Like the previous figure but made without the square base. Price A.

Figure 79.15. Midshipman. H: 8.1". On the same base as the following figure and figure 79.33, all probably being from the same pot bank. Other figures also occur on this base. Price B. *Collection of Arnold and Barbara Berlin.*

Figure 79.16. Midshipman. H: ~8.1". Price B.

Figure 79.17. Press ganger. H: 5.6". The baton and purse of coins identify the figure as a press ganger. Price A.

Figure 79.18. Sailor. H: ~9". Price A.

Figure 79.19. Sailor. H: 9.1". Price A. *Brighton and Hove Museums.*

Figure 79.20. Shipwrecked sailors, a pair. L: ~7.5", H: ~5.5". Flat on the back and can be placed back-to-back to form a circle. The right hand figure is recorded titled *The Shipwrecked Mariner.* Price B. *John Howard Antiques Woodstock, England.*

115

Figure 79.21. *THE POOR SOLDIER*. H: 6". A companion figure is titled *THE POOR LABORER* (Vol. 1, fig. 29.47). Price B.

Figure 79.22. *THE POOR SOLDIER*, reverse of previous figure.

Figure 79.23. The poor soldier. Attributed to "Sherratt." H: ~6". On a typical "Sherratt" base. Price A. *Brighton and Hove Museums.*

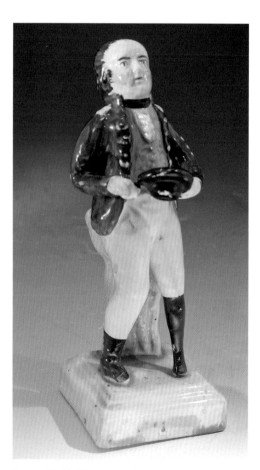

Figure 79.24. The poor soldier. H: 6". Price B. *John Howard; www.antiquepottery.co.uk.*

Figure 79.25. Amputee soldier. H: ~6". Price B. *Andrew Dando Antiques.*

Figure 79.26. Amputee soldier, reverse of previous figure. *Andrew Dando Antiques.*

Figure 79.27. Amputee soldier. H: 8.3". Price B. *Woolley and Wallis Salisbury Salerooms Ltd.*

Figure 79.28. Soldier attired as a Loyal Volunteer. H: ~6.5". Price B.

Figure 79.29. Soldier attired as a Loyal Volunteer. H: ~6.5". Price B.

Figure 79.30. Soldier attired as a Loyal Volunteer. Possibly made by Ralph Wood. H: ~7". The stoneware-type body coupled with blue lines on three sides of the base link this figure to others, all possibly by Ralph Wood. Price B. *Andrew Dando Antiques.*

Figure 79.31. Soldier attired as a Loyal Volunteer. H: ~6.5". Price B. *Andrew Dando Antiques.*

Figure 79.32. Soldier attired as a Loyal Volunteer. H: 8.3". Price B. *Andrew Dando Antiques.*

Figure 79.33. Soldier of the 80th Regiment of Foot (Staffordshire Volunteers). H: 8". Probably from the same pot bank as figures 79.15–16. Price B. *The William Herbert and Nancy Hunt Collection.*

Figure 79.34. Soldier, reverse of previous figure. Several other figures on this base appear to be from the same pot bank. *The William Herbert and Nancy Hunt Collection.*

Figure 79.35. Man holding sword. Attributed to "Sherratt." H: 5". Formed from the molds used for the figure of a tyler mason on large *PREPARE TO MEET THY GOD* groups (chapter 110). This figure also occurs on watch stands. Price A.

Figure 79.36. Man holding sword. Attributed to "Sherratt." H: ~5". The figure is painted to have a moustache, a quirky touch found also on some "Sherratt" shepherds. Price A.

Figure 79.37. Man holding sword. H: ~4.7". Price A.

Figures 79.38 through 79.41 portray Hessian soldiers, whose garb included blue coats, buff breeches, and distinctively pointed headgear. In the 1770s, King George III hired about 30,000 soldiers to fight for Britain in America. The men were all called Hessians because the largest group came from the German principality of Hesse-Kassel. The Hessians were highly respected fighters, and their regimental bands were admired. After the war, a Hessian band played at George Washington's inauguration. Britain contracted to bring 12,000 Hessians into the British army for four years from around 1793. And in 1798, Hessians put down a rebellion in Ireland. The figures are known only from these examples.

Figure 79.38. Hessian soldier playing a pipe. H: 8". Companion to the following two soldiers. Price D, set.

Figure 79.39. Hessian soldier playing a drum. H: 8". Companion to the previous and following soldier. Price D, set.

Figure 79.40. Hessian soldier playing a horn. H: 8". Companion to the previous two soldiers. Price D, set.

Figure 79.41. Hessian soldier, reverse of previous figure. The supports behind all three Hessian soldiers are from the same molds.

80. Slavery

In 1807, Britain's slave trade officially ended, but slavery continued in Britain's colonies until the Slavery Abolition Act abolished it from August 1, 1834. Figure 80.5, showing Britannia dancing with a liberated slave, was probably made to commemorate this landmark legislation. The figures of the kneeling slave (figs. 80.2–80.4) appear to predate emancipation and were perhaps made to support the abolitionist cause. Their design is reminiscent of the Slave Emancipation Society medallion that William Hackwood designed circa 1787, bearing the words "Am I not a man and a brother?" Perhaps Hackwood's design influenced these earthenware figures, but there may be some other as-yet-undiscovered design source.

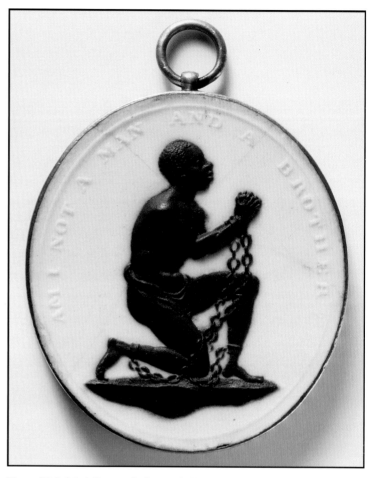

Figure 80.1. Medallion with the words "AM I NOT A MAN AND A BROTHER?" Such medallions were fashionable symbols of support for the abolitionist cause. © *Victoria and Albert Museum, London.*

Figure 80.2. Kneeling slave. H: 7". Price E.

Figure 80.3. Kneeling slave, previous figure, detail of the open book impressed "BLESS GOD THANK BRITTON ME NO SLAVE".

Figure 80.5. Liberated slave with Britannia. H: 7". Broken chains lie at the slave's feet. Made circa 1834 to celebrate the abolition of slavery in the English colonies. Known from only this example. Made without bocage. Price E. *John Howard; www.antiquepottery.co.uk.*

Figure 80.4. Kneeling slave. H: ~7". The open book is impressed "BLESS GOD THANK BRITTIN ME NO SLAVE". Price D.

121

Sport
81. Boxing

In the late eighteenth century, Britain's first sports stars rose to fame, and they were pugilists. These men were a source of national pride. That Englishmen distinguished themselves in a manly way with their bare fists (without any effete continental gestures) symbolized the nation's courage, strength, tenacity, and sense of fair play. Earthenware pugilists depict the epic battles of the sport's formative years: the contests between Thomas Cribb and Thomas Molineaux, and Thomas Spring and Jack Langan, battles in which Englishmen triumphed over boxers of other countries.[1]

In 1810, Thomas Molineaux, a freed American slave, challenged Thomas Cribb for England's boxing title. On December 18, the two men met in the rain before a huge crowd. Technically Molineaux won, but the thought of England's boxing crown going to either an American or a black man was so abhorrent that Molineaux was cheated of his victory, and Cribb was declared the winner. At a rematch on September 28, 1811, Cribb won decisively.

When Thomas Cribb retired as England's boxing champion, Thomas Spring (born Winter) stepped forward to claim the title. On January 7, 1824, Jack Langan, an Irishman, challenged Spring for the boxing crown. The men fought on an open race course before a crowd of 50,000 spectators. Spring won in seventy-seven rounds. On June 8, 1824, the men met again. After seventy-six rounds, and an hour and forty-nine minutes, Spring stretched forth his palm and humanely pushed an exhausted Langan to the turf. Spring retired after this fight because his hands could not withstand further pounding.

The Cribb- Molineaux and Spring-Langan fights were the events of their day. Engravings, prints, and paintings captured the pugilists and assisted in the modeling of the figures. Figures of Cribb and Molineaux were made by assorted pot banks into the Victorian era, and today crude Asian reproductions abound. Not shown here is a small group (about six inches tall) portraying Cribb and Molineaux on a simple oblong base and known from one example. The figure group portraying the Spring-Langan fight is particularly rare and is known from three examples, all with the Walton mark. Again crude copies of Asian origin are plentiful.

Figure 81.1. *Molineaux*, published by Robert Dighton, January 1812. © *Trustees of the British Museum.*

Figure 81.2. Thomas Cribb and Thomas Molineaux. H: 9" (L), 8.7" (R). These impressive figures, the bodies modeled with great attention to detail, probably date circa 1810. Price E. *John Howard; www.antiquepottery.co.uk.*

122

Figure 81.3. Thomas Cribb and Thomas Molineaux.
H: 8.5" (L), 8.7" (R). Price E.

Figure 81.4. Thomas Molineaux and Thomas Cribb. H: 8.5" (L), 8.4" (R).
Price E. *Collection of Arnold and Barbara Berlin.*

Figure 81.5. Thomas Cribb and Thomas Molineaux. H: 8.5" (L), 8.7" (R).
Price D. *Brighton and Hove Museums.*

Figure 81.6. Gentleman pugilist, perhaps Thomas
Cribb. H: ~8.5". An example of this figure paired
with Molineaux is recorded, and, for that reason, it
is thought to represent Cribb. However, this figure
also occurs paired with another formed from the
same molds. Price B.

Figure 81.7. Gentleman pugilist. H: 8".
May represent either Thomas Molineaux
or Bill Richmond, the African-American
pugilist who trained him. From the same
molds as the following two pugilists. Price
B. *Collection of Arnold and Barbara Berlin.*

Figure 81.8. Gentleman pugilist. H: 8.2". This
figure is sometimes said to represent Richard
Humphreys, although it bears no resemblance
to contemporary engravings of that famed
pugilist. Price B. *Brighton and Hove Museums.*

Figure 81.10. *SPRING, LANGAN.* Impressed
"WALTON". H: 7". Each pugilist's name is
impressed on a ribbon applied to his side of the
base. The Walton mark is on the reverse. Price F.

Figure 81.11. *SPRING, LANGAN,* previous example.

Figure 81.9. Gentleman pugilist.
H: ~8". Price B.

In the early days of boxing, women participated whole-heartedly in prize-fighting (or fighting merely to settle differences). In these no-holds-barred battles, women abandoned their stays and stripped to their slips. Each woman held coins or stones in her hands, and the first woman to drop these lost. Only one earthenware figure of a female pugilist is recorded. It is dubbed the Boxing Baroness because it is after a print titled thus. The Boxing Baroness was the name given to the notorious Lady Barrymore, wife of the fast-living Seventh Earl of Barrymore. Boxing was one of the Earl of Barrymore's particular pleasures, and he boxed with his wife, the former Miss Charlotte Goulding, until 1793, when his musket accidentally discharged and killed him. Lady Barrymore lived for many more years. Her obituary in the *Gentleman's Magazine* of 1832 reads, *"In Charles-court, Drury-lane, the notorious 'Lady Barrymore.' She had passed from the drawing-room of a profligate peer to the lowest grade of prostitution. She had been brought 150 times to Bow-street Office on charges of drunkenness and rioting, and possessed great pugilistic skill and strength; but, when kept sober in Tothill Fields Bridewell, proved an useful and trustworthy assistant of the female prisoners."*

Figure 81.13. Lady Barrymore, the Boxing Baroness. H: 7.1". Price B.

Figure 81.12. *The Boxing Baroness*, by Charles William for *Bon Ton Magazine*, March 1819.

82. Bear Baiting

Bear baiting was a contest that pitted tenacious dogs against a tethered bear, and spectators wagered on the outcome. The sport was at its height in the Elizabethan era but had waned by the 1800s because it had become less socially acceptable and because bears were in short supply. In 1835, bear baiting was banned. Bear baiting figures are particularly rare. Possibly print sources inspired them; possibly they mimic reality. The best-known figural forms are bear baiting jugs, and these have been crudely reproduced in recent years.

Figure 82.1. *The Country Squire taking a peep at Charley's Theatre Wesmr where the performers are of the Old School*, Henry Alken, circa 1820.

Figure 82.2. Bear baiting group. The dog baits a chained bear, and the bear keeper lies on the ground with his hat beside him. L: 13.5". The only recorded example of this group. Molds for the base, the man, and the bear were used in other groups. Price F.

Figure 82.3. Detail of previous bear baiting group.

126

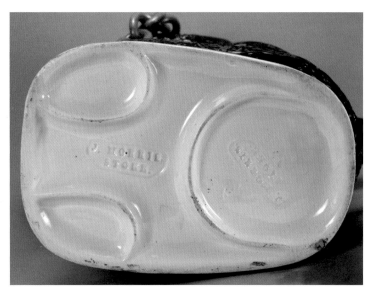

Figure 82.5. Bear baiting jug, previous example, with "J. MORRIS STOKE" impressed twice beneath.

Figure 82.4. Bear baiting jug. Impressed "J. MORRIS STOKE" twice beneath. H: 12.6". The bear's head lifts off to form a cup, and the dog's mouth is the spout. As the removable head is easily lost, this jug frequently occurs with a restored head. This head is original. Price E.

Figure 82.6. Bear baiting jug. H: 11.7". The head removes, and the dog's mouth is the jug's spout. Like the previous example, rarely found with the original head in place and intact. This head is original. Price E. *Newcastle-under-Lyme Museum.*

127

Figure 82.7. Napoleonic bear baiting jug, with the bear holding a monkey in French uniform caricaturing Napoleon. H: 10". In the Napoleonic Wars of 1803–1815. Bear baiting jugs with Napoleon in lieu of a dog ridiculed Napolean. The head of the jug is removable. Price E. *Bonhams.*

Figure 82.8. Bear baiting figure. The small dog clings tenaciously to the bear's jaw. H: 8.6". This figure does not serve as a jug. Price D. *Brighton and Hove Museums.*

Figure 82.9. Tobacco box with a dog baiting a bear serving as the knob of the lid. H: 7.5". Price C. *Collection of Arnold and Barbara Berlin.*

83. Bull Baiting

Bull baiting dates to the thirteenth century. Baiting a bull before slaughter was believed to tenderize its meat and drain poison from the animal's blood, and in the early 1800s, some communities still forbade the slaughter of a bull that had not been baited. Bull baiting was also a great gambling sport: wagers were placed on the dog's ability to pin the bull to the ground, while the bull tried to toss the dog into the air. Legislation of 1835 banned all baiting sports.

Today, vigorously styled bull baiting groups incorporating people are particularly popular, and reproductions of Asian origin are in circulation. Typically, these reproductions are significantly reduced in size and are after the "Sherratt" group titled *BULL BEATING, NOW CAPTIN LAD*. One small bull baiting that appears periodically on the market, described as early nineteenth century, was actually made in England in the first part of the twentieth century. This group is about seven inches long (Vol. 4, fig. 201.11). Anthony Oliver's *Staffordshire Potter: the Tribal Art of England*, pages 45 and 48, tells of this group being produced by the Kent factory as late as 1960. Oliver spoke to the man responsible for reducing the group from the Sherratt original. He was very proud of his derivative work and kept an example in a cabinet in his living room. Note that "Sherratt" did produce a small-scale bull baiting group, as shown in figures 83.12–13.

Groups portraying a lone dog baiting a bull are relatively common, and several pot banks made examples on this theme. Similar illustrations for John Gay's popular fable *The Bull and the Mastiff* probably influenced these figural groups.

Figure 83.1. *Bullbaiting*, Henry Alken, first published in 1822.

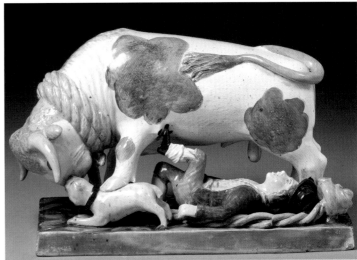

Figure 83.3. Bull baiting group. A man lying beside a dog and bull. L: 11.7". Price E. © *Victoria and Albert Museum, London.*

Figure 83.2. Bull baiting group. A man standing beside a dog and bull. L: ~11.5". A similar group is recorded with the base painted with a red and blue vermicular pattern. Price E. *John Howard; www. antiquepottery.co.uk.*

Figure 83.4. Bull baiting group. A man beside a bull and dog. L: 12". Price D. *The William Herbert and Nancy Hunt Collection.*

Figure 83.5. Bull baiting group. A man beside a bull and dog. L: 12.5". Price D.

Figure 83.6. Bull baiting group. A man beside a bull, another man beneath the bull, with two dogs. Attributed to "Sherratt." L: 13.8". "Sherratt" clawed bases appear to have been phased out by the later 1820s, and this group may predate the following "Sherratt" examples. Unlike them, it includes a man beneath the bull. Price E. © *Christie's Images Limited 2014.*

Figure 83.7. *BULL BEATING, NOW CAPTIN LAD*. A man with a bull and two dogs. Attributed to "Sherratt." H: 11.4", L: 14". This is the traditional, much-loved (and much-copied) "Sherratt" bull baiting, and word of mouth alone attributes it to Obadiah Sherratt. Occurs less commonly on a mound base. Price E.

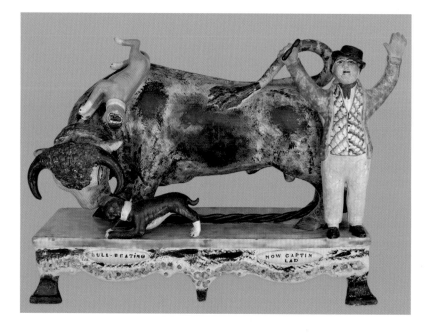

Figure 83.8. *BULL BEATING, NOW CAPTIN LAD*. A man with a bull and two dogs. Attributed to "Sherratt." L: 13.2". "Sherratt" bull baiting groups occur in assorted color palettes. The stick he holds is invariably damaged or restored. Price E. *Collection of Michael J. Smith.*

Figure 83.9. *BULL BEATING, NOW CAPTIN LAD*. A man with a bull and two dogs. Attributed to "Sherratt." H: 10.7", L: 13.2". Unlike the two previous similar examples, the man's hat is on the ground. Price E. *Nick Burton*.

Figure 83.10. Bull baiting group. A man with a bull and a dog. Attributed to "Sherratt." H: 8.5". Here the bull faces in the other direction, and the man is different. Price D.

Figure 83.11. *BULL BEATING*. A dog baiting a bull. Attributed to "Sherratt." L: 13.7". This group was made without a man. Price C. *Bonhams*.

Figure 83.12. Bull baiting group. A man with a bull and two dogs. Attributed to "Sherratt." H: 8", L: 9.5". The bull is smaller than that in larger groups previously shown. A rare group, not to be confused with reproductions of the traditional "Sherratt" group (Vol. 4, fig. 201.11). Price D. *Image courtesy of The Potteries Museum & Art Gallery, Stoke-on-Trent, UK*.

Figure 83.13. Bull baiting group. A man with a bull and two dogs. Attributed to "Sherratt." L: 8". Note the touches of pink luster as seen on "Sherratt" figures in particular. The bull is smaller than that in full-sized "Sherratt" groups. Price D. *Brighton and Hove Museums*.

Figure 83.14. Bull baiting group. A man with a bull and a dog. L: 17". This is the longest bull baiting group recorded. Price D. *Nick Burton.*

Figure 83.15. Dog baiting a bull. Attributed to "Sherratt." L: 8.5". The bull is smaller than the bull normally found on full-sized "Sherratt" bull baiting groups. Price C.

Figure 83.17. Dog baiting a bull, a cow with leg raised to avoid a snake, a pair, with bocages. H: ~7.5". These figures are rarely found paired and probably were originally sold as singles. Price D. *John Howard; www.antiquepottery.co.uk.*

Figure 83.16. Dog baiting a bull, with bocage. H: 7.5". Walton-style, but devoid of features to support an attribution. Price B. *Saffron Walden Museum.*

Figure 83.18. Dog baiting a bull, with bocage. H: 7.5". From the same pot bank as the previous bull but painted differently. Price B. *Dallas Auction Gallery.*

Figure 83.20. Dog baiting a bull, with bocage. Attributed to Hall. H: ~6.7". These six-petalled bocage flowers are characteristic of Hall. Price B.

Figure 83.21. Dog baiting a bull, with bocage. H: ~6.5". Note the leaves integral to the rim of the base. Price B.

Figure 83.19. Dog baiting a bull, with bocage. H: 6.5". The unusual bocage fronds are comprised of anthemion-type leaves arranged in threes. Price B.

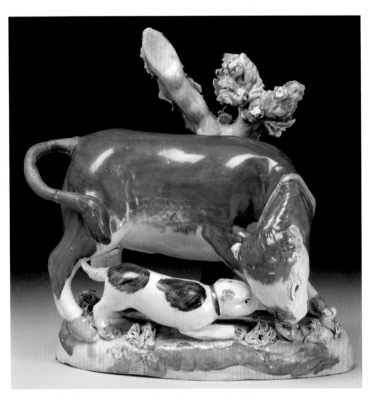

Figure 83.22. Dog baiting a bull, with bocage. L: 6.5".
Price B. © *Victoria and Albert Museum, London.*

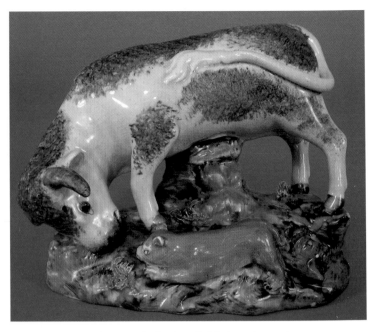

Figure 83.23. Dog baiting a bull. H: 5.5". Made without a bocage.
Price B. *Nick Burton.*

Figure 83.24. Dog baiting a bull. H: 5.5". Made without a bocage.
Price B. *Collection of Susan and Richard Cann.*

Figure 83.25. Dog baiting a bull, reverse of previous example.
Collection of Susan and Richard Cann.

Figure 83.26. Dog baiting a bull. "Thomas Hanshall July 1 1821" on the front of the base. Size not known. It is not known whether the mark (probably a maker's mark rather than a painter's mark) is scratched in the paint or inscribed in the body. Price D. *Andrew Dando Antiques.*

Figure 83.27. Dog baiting a bull. Size not known. The dog and bull are like those in the previous example. Both these groups are rare and desirable. Price D. *Andrew Dando Antiques.*

Figure 83.28. Dog baiting a bull before a spill vase. Possibly made by Ralph Wood. H: 10.5". The rainbow palette of the base is very suggestive of Ralph Wood. Price B. *Dallas Auction Gallery.*

Figure 83.29. Dog baiting a bull. L: 14". Price D. *John Howard; www.antiquepottery.co.uk.*

84. Archers, Sportsmen, Falconers, and Other Hunters

The late eighteenth century witnessed a revival of archery as a pastime for the upper classes. From the outset, newly formed archery clubs included women as full members. For ladies, archery was a rare opportunity to exercise with the opposite sex, and the sport's costumes and poses discreetly displayed a fine figure. Moreover, archery provided genteel exercise, and even older ladies could participate. Importantly, both sexes might share its conviviality. Gatherings of England's archery societies were grand social events resplendent with pageantry. Highly regulated conventions governed the minutest details of dress and etiquette.

Lady archers are the only female earthenware sporting figures. They can often be paired with figures of a gentleman shooting, sometimes titled *Sportsman*. Shooting, the term used to describe the pursuit of game on foot, was the ultimate gentleman's sport. Prior to 1831, the Game Act permitted only those with annual incomes from land of at least £100 per year to hunt game animals, such as hares, partridges, pheasant, and moorfowl. This law essentially gave rural landed gentry a monopoly on shooting for sport.

Archers and sportsmen may originally have been sold as single figures, and perhaps their initial purchasers paired them, or perhaps collectors assembled pairs subsequently. Today, figures of archers and sportsmen are plentiful, but a maker's mark, an unusual mold, or strong glaze and enameling can elevate a figure from mundane to superb. Other hunting figures and groups are much rarer, and the subject commands a price premium. Among them are groups depicting coursing, deer stalking, and falconry.

Figure 84.1. Lady archer and sportsman with dog, with bocage. H: 8.5". A rare group known from only this example. In the same style and with the same bocage as the dandies in volume 3, figure 133.23. Price C. *The William Herbert and Nancy Hunt Collection.*

Figure 84.2. Detail of the bocage on the previous example. Flowers are on some of the fronds and are painted green. *The William Herbert and Nancy Hunt Collection.*

Figure 84.3. Lady archer, with bocage. H: 7.5".
Attributed to "Sherratt." The floral sprigs applied
to the mound support the attribution, and the
anthemion bocage fronds and base are typical of
"Sherratt." Price B.

Figure 84.4. Lady archer, with bocage. H: 7.9".
Attributed to "Sherratt." Like the previous figure
but with different typical "Sherratt" bocage
fronds of oak leaflets with mayflowers. Price B.

Figure 84.5. Lady archer, with bocage. H: ~8".
Attributed to "Sherratt." Like the previous
figures but with a different mound atop the
base. This combination of bocage leaves
and flowers is characteristic of "Sherratt."
Companion to the next sportsman. Price B.

Figure 84.6. Sportsman with dog, with
bocage. H: 8". Attributed to "Sherratt."
The "Sherratt" sportsman is less common
than the archer. Companion to the
previous archer. Price B.

Figure 84.7. Sportsman with dog, lady archer, an assembled pair,
with bocages. Attributed to "Sherratt." His bocage is largely
restored. Both bocages have flowers not seen on the previous
"Sherratt" sportsmen and archers. Price B.

Figure 84.8. Lady archer, with bocage.
Attributed to "Sherratt." H: ~8".
Characteristic floral sprigs are applied
to the mound. The base is painted in
an atypical manner. The bocage has
five-leaflet fern fronds. Price A.

Figure 84.10. Sportsman with dog, lady archer, a pair, with bocages. Attributed to Patriotic Group. H: ~7.5". The bocage flowers are specific to the Patriotic Group, and the bocage leaves and the bases are consistent with the attribution. Price B.

Figure 84.9. Lady archer. Attributed to "Sherratt." H: ~7.1". Made without bocage. The floral sprigs applied to the mound are specific to "Sherratt." Price A.

Figure 84.11. Lady archer, with bocage. Attributed to Patriotic Group. H: 7.8". Like the previous archer from the same pot bank. The holly bocage is specific to the Patriotic Group. Price B. *Image courtesy of The Potteries Museum & Art Gallery, Stoke-on-Trent, UK.*

Figure 84.12. Lady archer, sportsman with dog, a pair. Possibly made by Enoch Wood. H: ~7". Made without bocages. Both have "27" impressed beneath in the manner of Enoch Wood, but the figures lack features to confirm attribution. Price B.

Figure 84.13. Sportsman with dog, two figures. H: ~7". Made without bocages. The mounds are formed from different molds. Price A each.

Figure 84.16. Sportsman with dog, lady archer, a pair, with bocages. Probably made by Enoch Wood. H: ~7". The bocages (seven-leaflet fern fronds) and bases together suggest the attribution. Price B.

Figure 84.14. Archer. H: ~7". Possibly made by Enoch Wood. The mounded base is in the style of Enoch Wood. The bocage is lost. From the same molds as the archer in figure 84.12. Price A.

Figure 84.15. Sportsman with dog. Possibly made by Enoch Wood. H: 7". Impressed "KK" beneath. The base is in the style of Enoch Wood, and workers' marks are sometimes impressed beneath Enoch Wood bases. Bocage probably lost. Price A.

Figure 84.17. Lady archer, sportsman, a pair, with bocages. Probably made by Enoch Wood. H: ~7". His bocage (hawthorn fronds) is typical of Enoch Wood. Her bocage is restored. The dog usually with the sportsman may have been omitted but is more often lost. Price A.

Figure 84.18. Sportsman with dog, lady archer, a pair. Possibly made by Enoch Wood. H: ~5". Significantly smaller figures than the previous pairs, with restored bocages and typical Enoch Wood bases. Price A.

Figure 84.19. Sportsman with dog, with bocage. Probably made by Enoch Wood. H: 7". The base and bocage are both typical of Enoch Wood, and this figure occurs with other Enoch Wood-style bocages. Price A.

Figure 84.20. Sportsman with dog, with bocage. Attributed to Dale. H: 8". The bocage leaves and flowers support the attribution. The bocage fits into a socket, and this is another Dale feature. Price B.

Figure 84.21. Sportsman with dog, reverse of previous figure. When a bocage is made in this way, it is usually possible to lift it from the socket. Here the glazes melded in firing, fixing the bocage within the socket.

Figure 84.22. Sportsman, with bocage. Attributed to Dale. H: ~8". Bocage restored; dog possibly lost. The large floral sprigs on the base are characteristic of Dale. Price A.

Figure 84.23. Sportsman with dog, with bocage. Probably made by Dale. H: 8.5". Like previous Dale examples. The bocage and its flowers are consistent with attribution. Price B.

Figure 84.24. Sportsman, with bocage. Attributed to Dale. H: 8.5". The eight-petalled bocage flowers support the attribution. A dog may have been lost from the base. Price A.

Figure 84.25. Lady archer. Attributed to Dale. H: ~7". Bocage lost. The floral sprigs on the base are characteristic of Dale. Price A.

Figure 84.26. Sportsman with dog, lady archer, a pair. Possibly made by Dale. H: ~7". Bocages restored. The figures and bases are from Dale molds, and, although the flowers on the base are non-specific, a Dale attribution is possible. Price A.

Figure 84.27. Sportsman with dog, lady archer, a pair, bocages lost. H: ~7". A strongly enameled pair lacking features for attribution. Like many other archers, she has a dress pattern suggestive of archery targets. Price A.

141

Figure 84.28. Lady archer, sportsman with dog, a pair, with bocages. H: ~6". These three leaflets bocage fronds occur on related figures as yet unclassified. Price B.

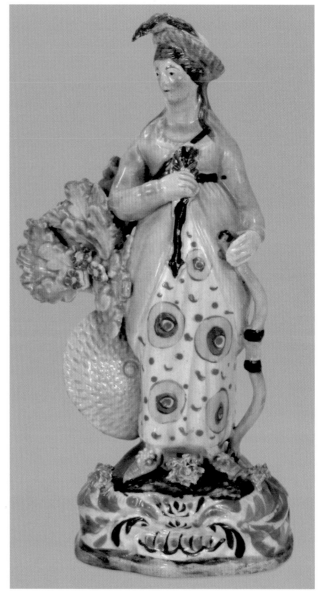

Figure 84.29. Lady archer, with bocage. H: ~6". Like the previous archer and probably from the same pot bank, but with a different bocage. Large archery targets are painted on her dress. Price A.

Figure 84.30. Detail of bocage on the previous lady archer.

Figure 84.31. Lady archer, with bocage. H: ~6". Like the previous archer but with a different bocage (restored), now placed on the other side. Price A.

Figure 84.32. Lady archer. H: ~6". Made without bocage. Probably from the same pot bank as the previous three archers. Price A.

Figure 84.33. Sportsman with dog, lady archer, a pair, with bocages. Attributed to Tunstall Group. H: ~6.5". The bocages have carnations as well as distinctive "Tunstall" flowers. Price B.

Figure 84.34. Lady archer, with bocage. Attributed to Tunstall Group. H: ~6.2". Like the previous archer and with bocage flowers that are specific to the Tunstall Group. Price A.

Figure 84.35. Lady archer, with bocage. Attributed to Tunstall Group. H: 6.2". The base and the lady's head and bow differ from those of the previous figure. The bocage leaves and flowers support the attribution. Price A. *Elinor Penna.*

Figure 84.36. Sportsman with dog, with bocage. Attributed to the Tunstall Group. H: 6.7". On the same D-shaped base as the previous archer and with bocage fronds and flowers that support the attribution. Price A.

Figure 84.37. Lady archer, with bocage. Possibly attributable to Tunstall Group. H: 6". From the same figure molds as the Tunstall archer in figure 84.35, but with an arrow in her hand. Price A.

Figure 84.38. *SPORTSMAN* (title faintly impressed), with dog, with bocage. H: ~7". In the Salt style but not necessarily made by Salt. Price A.

Figure 84.39. *SPORTSMAN* (title faintly impressed), with dog, with bocage. Impressed "SALT". H: ~7". Price A.

Figure 84.40. Sportsman, with dog, with bocage. H: 6.9". Like the previous sportsman marked "SALT" but unmarked. Salt figures have no specific features, so only a mark can establish an attribution. Loss of or restoration to the outstretched hand is common on examples of this figure. Price A.

Figure 84.41. *SPORTS MAN*, with dog, with bocage. Impressed "SALT". H: 7". Pairs with the following *ARCHAR*. Price B. *Elinor Penna.*

Figure 84.42. *ARCHAR*, with bocage. Impressed "SALT". H: 6.6". Pairs with the previous sportsman. Pink clothing occurs surprisingly frequently on Salt figures, as do fat flower stalks beneath the carnations. Price B.

Figure 84.43. *ARCHAR* (title partially impressed), with bocage. Impressed "SALT". H: ~6.8". Like the previous archer. The flame-like pattern on the lower skirt can be observed on other Salt figures. Price B.

Figure 84.44. Archer, with bocage. H: ~7". Very like the previous Salt archers but unmarked. Pairs with the unmarked sportsman in figure 84.40. Price A.

Figure 84.45. Archer, with bocage. H: 7". The bocage flowers are not the carnations typically found on other Salt look-alikes. Price A. *Elinor Penna.*

Figure 84.46. Archer, with bocage. H: ~5.5". An uncommon figure. This base and these unusual bocage fronds occur on a pair of gardeners (Vol. 1, fig. 24.101). Price A.

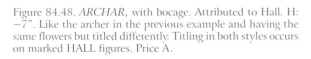

Figure 84.47. *SPORTSMAN, ARCHAR*, with bocages. Attributed to Hall. H: ~7". The bocage flowers are characteristic of Hall, and the sloppy titling is seen most frequently on Hall figures. Price B.

Figure 84.48. *ARCHAR*, with bocage. Attributed to Hall. H: ~7". Like the archer in the previous example and having the same flowers but titled differently. Titling in both styles occurs on marked HALL figures. Price A.

Figure 84.49. *ARCHAR*, with bocage. Attributed to Hall. H: 6.6". This six-petalled flower is specific to Hall. Price A. *Michael Goodacre.*

Figure 84.50. *ARCHAR*, with bocage. Attributed to Hall. H: ~7". Like previous Hall archers. The painting of the bocage acorns, the tooling of the leaves, and the titling support the attribution. Price A.

Figure 84.51. Sportsman with dog, lady archer, an assembled pair, with bocages. Both marked "WALTON". H: ~6.4" (L), ~6.9" (R). Price B.

Figure 84.52. Archer, with bocage. H: 7". Unusual in the placement of the bocage. Price A.

Figure 84.53. Sportsman with dog, with bocage. H: ~5". On the bocage, only the lower right frond is original. Price A.

Figure 84.54. Sportsman with dog, with bocage. H: ~6". An unusual figure with triple-hawthorn bocage fronds. Price A.

Figure 84.55. Archer, with bocage. Attributed to Leather Leaf Group. H: ~7". Bocage restored. The flowers on the base establish the attribution. Price A.

Figure 84.56. *Sportsman, & Lady* Sportsman and lady holding a bird, a pair, each with a dog and bocage. Attributed to Ralph Wood. H: 7.5". The lady also occurs impressed "48"; the sportsman occurs in colored glazes impressed "47". Price B.

Figure 84.57. *Sportsman*, with dog, with bocage. Attributed to Ralph Wood. H: ~8". The bocage is restored. The titling and painting of the base support the attribution. Price A.

Figure 84.58. *Sportsman*, with dog, with bocage. Attributed to Dudson. H: ~7.5". With a typical Dudson bocage and titling. Price A.

Figure 84.59. *Mate*. Lady holding a bird, with a dog, with bocage. Attributed to Dudson. H: ~7.5". Pairs with previous sportsman. Dudson x-sprigs are on the base. Price A.

Figure 84.60. Sportsman with dog, with bocage. Marked "WALTON". H: ~6". Bocage restored. Price A.

Figure 84.61. Sportsman with dog, lady reading and with a cat, a pair, with bocages. He is attributed to Walton; she with an illegible Walton ribbon on the reverse. H: ~6". Normally, unmarked figures cannot be attributed to Walton, but the similarity to the previous sportsman supports the attribution. Price B. *Collection of Susan and Richard Cann.*

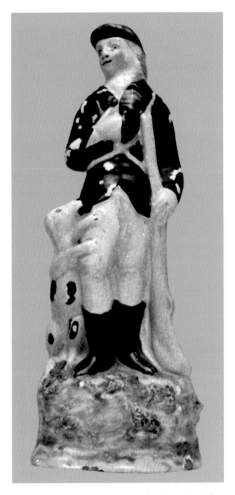

Figure 84.62. Sportsman with dog. H: ~5".
Made without bocage. Price A.

Figure 84.63. Sportsman. H: ~5". The bocage is unusual, as is the octagonal base. Price A.

Figure 84.64. Sportsman, to the right, with dog, with bocage. Impressed "WALTON". H: 6.5". Part of a garniture. Price C.

Figure 84.65. Sportsman, to the left, with bocage. Impressed "WALTON". H: ~6.5". The Walton sportsman facing left never has a dog, while the similar sportsman facing right routinely does, as seen in the previous example. Price B.

Figure 84.66. Four-piece sporting garniture. All impressed "WALTON". H: ~6.5" max. Walton sporting figures can assemble into a garniture comprising as many as six pieces. In addition to those shown, a group of two small dogs and a group of pheasants is recorded (fig. 84.67 and Vol. 3, fig. 113.73). Price E.

Figure 84.67. Four-piece sporting garniture. All impressed "WALTON". H: 6.5" max. This garniture includes a group of two small dogs rather than the hare in the previous example. Price E. *Jonathan Horne.*

Figure 84.68. Sportsman, dog, and game birds, with bocage. H: 7.2". Shooting groups with bocages are rare and desirable. Price E. *Nick Burton.*

Figure 84.69. Sportsman, dog, and game birds, with bocage. L: 7". Price D. *Jonathan Horne.*

Figure 84.70. Sportsman, dog, and hare, with spill vase. H: 7". Price A.

Figure 84.71. Sportsman, dog, and game bird, with spill vase. H: 7". Price A.

Figure 84.72. Sportsman and dog, with spill vase. H: 7". In the same style as previous examples, with loss of a small animal from the base. Price A.

Figure 84.73. Sportsman with dog, hare, and birds, with bocage. Possibly made by Dale. H: 9". The bocage fits into the socket. With restorations and possible loss of a small fox. Price B.

Figure 84.74. Sportsman with dog, fox, hare, and birds, with bocage. Possibly made by Dale. H: 8.6". The tall bocage that once fitted into the socket is lost. Price C. *Photograph Courtesy of Sotheby's, Inc. © 2014.*

Figure 84.75. Deer stalker with dog, with bocage. Attributed to "Sherratt." H: 7.7". Deer stalking is a long-established Scottish pursuit. A rare figure, known from three examples. Later look-alikes persisted into the twentieth century. Price C.

Figure 84.76. Deer stalker with dog. Attributed to "Sherratt." H: 7.6". Possibly from the same design source as a transfer printed figure on plates made by William Adams & Sons as part of their Caledonia pattern series. Price C.

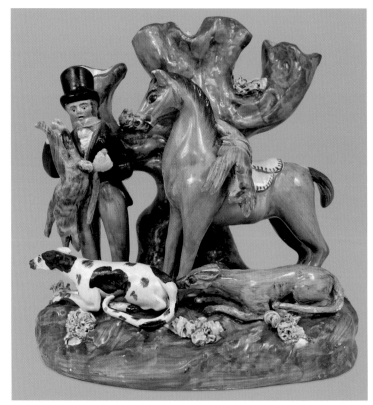

Figure 84.77. Coursing group. Gentleman holding a hare, with a horse and two greyhounds, with spill vase. H: 6.5". Price D. *Brighton and Hove Museums.*

Figure 84.78. Coursing group. Gentleman holding a hare, with a horse and two greyhounds, with spill vase. H: ~6.5". Like the previous example but painted differently. Price D. *The Moore Collection.*

Figure 84.79. Coursing group. Gentleman holding a hare, with a horse, with spill vase. Possibly attributable to Leather Leaf Group. H: ~6.5". The painting and flowers suggest the attribution. Price C.

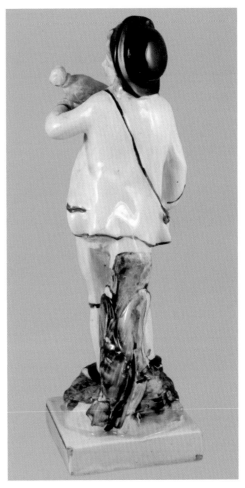

Figure 84.80. *Falconer.* Gentleman falconer holding a bird. Attributed to Ralph Wood. H: 9.1". Made without bocage. This figure also occurs impressed "135". Price B. *The William Herbert and Nancy Hunt Collection.*

Figure 84.81. *Falconer,* reverse of previous figure. *The William Herbert and Nancy Hunt Collection.*

Figure 84.82. Gentleman falconer with bird. H: 8.1". Made without bocage and without a square base. After a similar Derby figure of a gentleman holding a cockerel, introduced circa 1765. Price B.

Figure 84.83. Gentleman falconer, reverse of previous figure.

Figure 84.84. Gentleman falconer with bird, with bocage. H: ~8". Made without a square base. Like the previous figure but with bocage added. Price A.

Figure 84.85. Gentleman falconer with bird. H: 8". Made without bocage fronds. Price A. *Andrew Dando Antiques.*

154

Figure 84.86. Gentleman falconer with bird, with bocage. H 9.5". The bird and the man's neck clothing differ slightly from previous examples. The base is painted in an unusual manner, and the blue lines on it are uncommon. Price B. *Image courtesy of The Potteries Museum & Art Gallery, Stoke-on-Trent, UK.*

Figure 84.87. Gentleman falconer with bird. H: ~9.5". From the same molds as the previous falconer but apparently made without a bocage. Price A.

Figure 84.88. *Gamekeeper.* A gamekeeper with his gun and dog. H: 8.6". Made without bocage. This figure occurs impressed "36" (Colonial Williamsburg 1963-574). Price A. *The William Herbert and Nancy Hunt Collection.*

Figure 84.89. *Gamekeeper,* reverse of previous example. *The William Herbert and Nancy Hunt Collection.*

155

Bible and Religion
85. Abraham Offering Isaac

The well-known story in Genesis of the binding of Isaac is powerfully symbolic. At God's command, Abraham raises his knife to slay his beloved son, Isaac, but God stays Abraham's hand and presents instead a sacrificial ram. This tale's compelling message of paternal authority, filial duty, and faith in a higher order has been portrayed in classical art for centuries, and an old masters' print (probably after Rembrandt) or a derivative work may have inspired the earthenware figure groups.

Figure 85.2. Abraham offering Isaac, with bocage. H: ~10.3". Like the previous example but with a different bocage. Price B. *Collection of Michael J. Smith.*

Figure 85.1. Abraham offering Isaac, with bocage. H: 10.1". With a Salt-style bocage. The impressed inscription on the plinth supporting the amphora is from Genesis and reads "GEN XXII VARS 10 ABRAHAM STRETCHED FORTH HIS HAND AND TOOK THE KNIFE TO SLAY HIS SON". Price B.

Figure 85.3. Abraham offering Isaac, with bocage. H: ~10.3". Like the previous examples but with a quite different bocage. Price B.

Figure 85.4. Abraham offering Isaac, with bocage. Attributed to Patriotic Group. H: 10". The words on the rock beneath Isaac read "GENESIS CHAP 22 ABRAHAM OFFERING UP ISAAC". This base is less common than the bases on the following examples from the same pot bank. Price B. *Collection of Michael J, Smith.*

Figure 85.5. Abraham offering Isaac, with bocage. Attributed to Patriotic Group. H: 10.5". Like the previous example but upon a more typical Patriotic Group base. Note the misspelling, "OFEERING". Price B.

Figure 85.6. Abraham offering Isaac, with bocage. Attributed to Patriotic Group. H: ~11". Price B. *John Howard; www.antiquepottery.co.uk.*

Figure 85.7. Abraham offering Isaac, with bocage. Attributed to Patriotic Group. H: ~10". Like previous examples but with a hawthorn bocage. Price B.

Figure 85.8. Abraham offering Isaac, with bocage. Attributed to Patriotic Group. H: ~11". Painted in turquoise rather than green, as sometimes occurs on Patriotic Group figures. Price B.

Figure 85.9. Abraham offering Isaac, with bocage. Attributed to Patriotic Group. H: 11". Like previous examples but with a less common fern bocage. Price B.

Figure 85.10. Abraham offering Isaac, with angel, with bocage. H: ~14". Note the angel (with restoration). Other examples on similar colorfully painted bases probably each originally had an angel perched atop. Price B.

Figure 85.11. Abraham offering Isaac, with bocage. H: 13.6". Like the previous example but with a different bocage and lacking the angel and small lamb. The base is painted differently and with great attention to detail. Price B. *Collection of Arnold and Barbara Berlin.*

Figure 85.12. *ABRAHAM OFFERING HIS SON ISAAC*, with bocage. H: 13.2". With losses. Like previous examples but titled. Price B. *Image courtesy of The Potteries Museum & Art Gallery, Stoke-on-Trent, UK.*

Figure 85.13. *ABRAHAM OFFERING HIS SON ISAAC*, with bocage. H: ~13.3". Like the previous example, but with different bocage fronds (with restoration). An angel may be lost from atop the bocage. Price B.

Figure 85.14. *ABRAM STOP*. Abraham offering Isaac, with a large angel, with bocage. Attributed to "Sherratt." H: ~12". Price C.

Figure 85.15. *ABRAM STOP*. Abraham offering Isaac, with a large angel, with bocage. Attributed to "Sherratt." H: 11.4". This group also occurs on a similarly shaped marbled table base. Price C.

Figure 85.16. *ABRAHAM STOP*. Abraham offering Isaac, with a large angel, with bocage. H: 11.2". Attributed to "Sherratt." Price C. *Elinor Penna.*

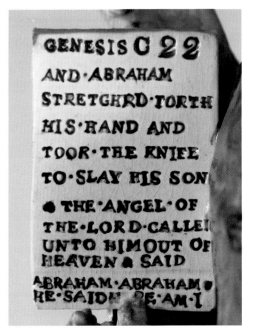

Figure 85.17. Detail of tablet on previous example impressed "GENESIS C 22 AND ABRAHAM STRETGHRD FORTH HIS HAND AND TOOR THE KNIFE TO SLAY HIS SON THE ANGEL OF THE LORD CALLED UNTO HIM OUT OF HEAVEN & SAID ABRAHAM ABRAHAM HE SAID HERE AM I". *Elinor Penna.*

Figure 85.18. *ABRAHAM STOP*. Abraham offering Isaac, with a large angel, with bocage. Attributed to "Sherratt." H: 13". The tablet reads as on the previous example. Also occurs on a brown clawed base with the tablet in the center front. Price C. *Brighton and Hove Museums.*

Figure 85.19. Abraham offering Isaac, with bocage. H: 7.3". The plaque to the side reads "HE SAID LAY NOT THINE AND UPON THE LAD NEITHER DO THOU ANY THING UNTO HIM". Price B. *Image courtesy of The Potteries Museum & Art Gallery, Stoke-on-Trent, UK.*

Figure 85.20. Abraham offering Isaac, with bocage. H: 7.2". Like the previous example but with a different bocage. Rembrandt shows an angel hovering over Abraham, and derivative prints probably influenced such figure groups. Price B.

Figure 85.21. Abraham offering Isaac, with bocage. H: ~7.5". Like the prior two examples but with cilantro bocage leaves. All three examples may originate from the same pot bank. Price B.

86. Jesus and Nicodemus

The *Gospel of John* tells that Nicodemus, a Pharisee and member of the Sanhedrin, visited Jesus by night to hear his teachings. Depictions of Jesus's instruction of Nicodemus have been popular in art for centuries, and an image probably influenced earthenware figures of Jesus and Nicodemus. All recorded examples are attributable to the Patriotic Group. Nicodemus has a triangular tablet impressed "CHRIST TEACHETH NICODEMUS JOHN 3 CH 3". Jesus's foot rests on a box impressed "CHRIST TEACHETH JOHN 3 CH 3", and the tablet in his hands (frequently lost) reads "MARVEL NOT THAT I SAID UNTO THEE YE MUST BE BORN AGAIN"

Figure 86.1. Jesus (L) and Nicodemus (R), a pair with bocages. Attributed to Patriotic Group. H: ~11" max. The bases and bocages are typical of this Group. Both figures have restored hands, and Jesus probably held a tablet that is now lost. Price B, pair.

Figure 86.2. Jesus, with bocage. Attributed to Patriotic Group. H: 10.9". Like the previous example, but with a different bocage that is also characteristic of the Group. Pairs with the next figure of Nicodemus. Restored tablet. Price B. *Elinor Penna.*

Figure 86.3. Nicodemus, with bocage. Attributed to Patriotic Group. Pairs with the previous figure of Jesus. H: ~10.7". Price B. *Elinor Penna.*

Figure 86.4. Nicodemus. Attributed to Patriotic Group. H: 10.9". Like previous figures but with cilantro bocage fronds. Price B.

87. Jesus and the Woman of Samaria

The *Gospel of John* tells that Jesus, weary from his travels, stops at Jacob's well to rest. There he meets the Woman of Samaria, drawing water at the well. Early artworks depicting this subject copy Michelangelo's painting, circa 1540, and the theme recurs in early nineteenth-century prints. Figure groups of this subject are rare. All are made by "Sherratt," with the exception of an apparently unique pair in the Brighton and Hove Museums.

Figure 87.2. Jesus and the Woman of Samaria. H: 7.4". This group showing Jesus resting at the well pairs with the following group and is known only from this example. Price B. *Brighton and Hove Museums.*

Figure 87.1. Jesus and the Woman of Samaria, with bocage. Attributed to "Sherratt." H: 8". Price C. *Brunk Auctions, Asheville, North Carolina.*

Figure 87.3. Jesus and the Woman of Samaria. H: 6.3". Pairs with the previous group and is known only from this example. Both were made without bocages. Price B. *Brighton and Hove Museums.*

Figure 87.4. Jesus and the Woman of Samaria, reverse of previous example. *Brighton and Hove Museums.*

88. Jesus in the Garden of Gethsemane

Entering the garden of Gethsemane and knowing his arrest is imminent, Jesus prays sorrowfully, "My Father, if it be possible, let this cup pass from Me." (*Gospels of Matthew 26:36–56; Mark 14:32–52; Luke 22:40–53; John 18:1–12*). Images of this scene have been popular in art for centuries and probably inspired the earthenware figures below. The figures are sometimes referred to as *Christ's Agony* or *Jesus Praying*, and some are titled thus. Sometimes lengthier titling references the passing of the cup.

Figure 88.1. *O MY FATHER LET THIS CUP PASS FROM ME*. Jesus in the Garden of Gethsemane, with angel, with bocage. Attributed to "Sherratt." H: 11.5". The blue "Sherratt" table base is rare, but the form of the base and the floral sprigs on the mound support attribution. Price B. *Brunk Auctions, Asheville, North Carolina*.

Figure 88.2. *O MY FATHER LET THIS CUP PASS FROM ME*. Jesus in the Garden of Gethsemane, with angel, with bocage. Attributed to "Sherratt." H: 12.1". Like the previous figure but with the anthemion bocage fronds "Sherratt" used. Price B. *Brighton and Hove Museums*.

Figure 88.3. *O MY FATHER LET THIS CUP PASS FROM ME*. Jesus in the Garden of Gethsemane, with angel, with bocage. Attributed to "Sherratt." H: ~12". Bocage restored. The mound sports a particularly splendid array of characteristic "Sherratt" sprigs and clusters of flowers normally on bocages. Price B. *Collection of Michael J. Smith*.

Figure 88.4. *CHRISTS AGONY.* Jesus in the Garden of Gethsemane, with angel, with bocage. Attributed to "Sherratt." H: 9.9". A typical "Sherratt" base and bocage. Price B.

Figure 88.5. Detail of the previous *CHRISTS AGONY.* The wording impressed on the plinth beneath the angel reads "FATHER LET THIS CUP PASS".

Figure 88.6. Jesus in the Garden of Gethsemane, with angel, with bocage. Attributed to "Sherratt." H: ~11". Uses the same figure molds as previous examples. The clusters of three flowers (formed together in one mold) on the base and bocage are a "Sherratt" feature. Price B.

Figure 88.7. *FATHER IF THOU BE WILLING REMOVE THIS CUP.* Jesus in the Garden of Gethsemane, with bocage. Attributed to Dale. H: ~9". A characteristic Dale floral sprig is on the base. Typical Dale bocage and color palette. Price B.

Figure 88.8. *FATHER, IF THOU BE WILLING REMOVE THIS CUP.* Jesus in the Garden of Gethsemane, with angel, with bocage. Attributed to Dale. H: 8". Like the previous example but heavily strewn with the eight-petalled bocage flowers and floral sprigs characteristic of Dale. Price B.

Figure 88.9. *JESUS PRAYING.* Jesus in the Garden of Gethsemane, with angel, with bocage. H: 7.5". Note the large halo. All but the central two bocage fronds are restored. Probably from the same pot bank as the following two examples. Price A.

Figure 88.10. *JESUS PRAYING*. Jesus in the Garden of Gethsemane, with angel, with bocage. H: ~8". Hawthorn bocage fronds are distinctive, but their use was not confined to one pot bank. Like the previous and following examples and titled in the same manner. Price B.

Figure 88.11. *JESUS PRAYING*. Jesus in the Garden of Gethsemane, with angel, with bocage. H: ~8.5". Like the previous two examples but with a different cherub and with sheep on the base. The bocage fronds are as on the previous example. Price B.

Figure 88.12. Jesus in the Garden of Gethsemane, with bocage. Attributed to Leather Leaf Group. H: ~8". The leaves and flowers on the base, the bocage flowers, and the distinctive painting of the base are characteristic of this Group. An angel is probably lost. Price A.

Figure 88.13. Jesus in the Garden of Gethsemane, with angel, with bocage. Attributed to Leather Leaf Group. H: ~9.5". Like the previous example, but here the bocage flowers have four petals rather than five. Price B.

Figure 88.14. Jesus in the Garden of Gethsemane, with angel, with bocage. Attributed to Leather Leaf Group. H: 9.5". Like the previous example but with curled leaves (a Leather Leaf feature) added to the bocage. Price B. *Richard F. Deloache, Dallas, Texas.*

89. Crucifixion

Figures portraying the crucifixion of Jesus are uncommon. All known bocage groups are of the same form, and older books routinely attribute examples to Walton. It has been impossible to verify the existence of a single marked Walton example, and all bocage examples are believed to be unmarked.[1]

The figure of the Pieta is particularly rare, and is almost certainly modeled after a smaller copy of one of Europe's famous sculptures.

Figure 89.1. The crucifixion of Jesus, with bocage. H: 10". Price C. *John Howard; www.antiquepottery.co.uk.*

Figure 89.2. The Pieta. Attributed to Enoch Wood; impressed "Nº 6" on the back of the base. H: 8.2". Matches the following excavated figure. A similar figure in the Earle Collection (#529) is impressed and painted "*N. S. DA PIEDADE.*" Price B.

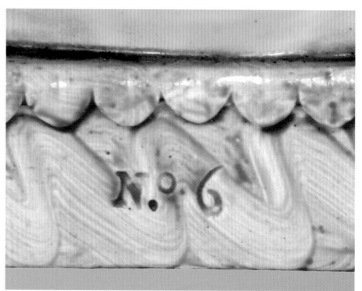

Figure 89.3. The impressed "No. 6" on the back of the previous figure.

Figure 89.4. The Pieta. Attributed to Enoch Wood; impressed "No. 6" on the back of the base. H: 8.2". This partial figure was excavated from the Burslem Old Town Hall site associated with Enoch Wood circa 1825. *Image courtesy of The Potteries Museum & Art Gallery, Stoke-on-Trent, UK.*

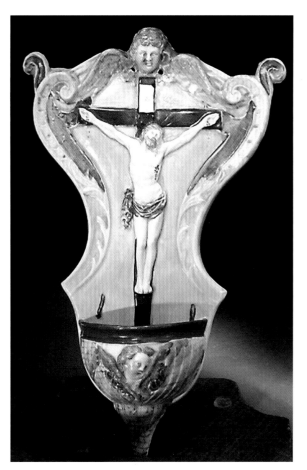

Figure 89.5. Stoup portraying the crucifixion of Jesus. H: 11". Price A. *John Howard; www.antiquepottery.co.uk.*

Figure 89.6. Stoup portraying the crucifixion of Jesus. H: 11". Price A.

Figure 89.7. Stoup portraying the crucifixion of Jesus. H: 6.2". Price A. *Elinor Penna.*

90. Elijah and the Widow

Elijah was a ninth century B.C.E. Old Testament prophet. In *First Kings*, Elijah flees Israel, and God tells him to hide by a brook. Here a miracle happens, and ravens feed Elijah. When the brook dries up, God sends Elijah to Zarephath, where he asks a widow for food. The widow does not have enough food for herself and her son, but Elijah promises that her jar of flour and jug of oil will not run dry. The miracle is fulfilled, and the food is replenished. Although the two miracles are two biblical tales, Staffordshire potters combined them within one figure pair: Elijah is usually portrayed with ravens, representing the miracle of his nourishment; the Widow of Zarephath usually has vessels of food and is portrayed with her son. These tales of Elijah were represented in old master paintings, and prints probably influenced the creation of the earthenware figures. The earliest figure models on this theme were made by Ralph Wood, circa 1790, and in ensuing decades other pot banks fashioned figures in much the same style. A multitude of extant examples by very many pot banks attest to the popularity of the subject in the 1790–1830 period.

Figure 90.1. *WIDDOW 1 KINGS CHAP 17 ELIJAH*. Elijah and the Widow, a watch stand with bocage. Attributed to Leather Leaf Group. H: ~11.7". The only recorded widow and Elijah on a common base. The bocage flowers are characteristic of the Group. Price B.

Figure 90.2. Widow, with bocage. Attributed to Leather Leaf Group. H: ~9.5". Like the widow in the previous example and with characteristic leaves and flowers on the base and bocage. Price A.

Figure 90.3. Widow, with bocage. Attributed to Leather Leaf Group. H: ~9.8". Like the previous figure but with acorns and "leathery" curled bocage leaves that give this group its name. Price A. *www.madelena.com.*

Figure 90.4. Elijah, with bocage. Attributed to Leather Leaf Group. H: ~11". Characteristic flowers and the base support the attribution. Price A.

Figure 90.5. *Widow of Sarepta, Elijah*, a pair, with bocages. Attributed to Ralph Wood. *Elijah* impressed "169"; *Widow of Sarepta* impressed "170". H: 11". With losses. Ralph Wood figures are probably the earliest examples of this subject. This is the only recorded widow impressed "170". Price A. *Angus Northeast.*

Figure 90.6. *Elijah*, with bocage. Attributed to Ralph Wood. H: 11". Unnumbered but like the figure that occurs impressed "169". Price A.

Figure 90.7. *Widow*, with bocage. Attributed to Ralph Wood. H: 10.3". Like the figure impressed "170" but made without a child. Several other examples of this figure attributed to Ralph Wood and made without the child have been documented. Price A. © *Victoria and Albert Museum, London.*

Figure 90.8. *Elijah*, with bocage. Attributed to Ralph Wood. H: 10.1". Like the previous Ralph Wood examples but with different yet typical titling and painting. Titling in this script occurs on Ralph Wood figures painted in a muddier palette. Price A. © *Victoria and Albert Museum, London.*

Figure 90.9. Elijah. Probably made by Ralph Wood. H: ~9.8". Made without bocage. The painted line bands three sides of the base. A companion widow with the base similarly painted is recorded. Price A.

Figure 90.10. Elijah and the widow, a pair. Possibly made by Enoch Wood. H: ~9.8". Made without bocages. The widow's jug is lost. This model of Elijah matches excavated Enoch Wood fragments. Price A.

Figure 90.11. Widow. H: 9.7". Made without bocage. Painted in a typical late eighteenth-century palette. Price A. *Brighton and Hove Museums.*

Figure 90.12. Widow. H: 9". A less common variation. Price A. *Barbara Gair; www.castle-antiques.com.*

Figure 90.13. Elijah, with bocage. Attributed to Big Blossom Group. H: ~10.2". The flowers are characteristic of the Group, and these bocage fronds occur on other figures from the same pot bank. Price A.

Figure 90.14. Elijah, with bocage. Attributed to Big Blossom Group. H: 10.2". Triple lines on bases are an unusual decorative feature. Price A.

Figure 90.15. *Widow*, with bocage. Attributed to Dudson. H: 10.2". The bocage, the base, and the titling are typical of Dudson. Price A. *The Bowes Museum, Barnard Castle.*

Figure 90.18. Base of the previous *Elijah* formed in the manner of Dudson bases. *Elinor Penna.*

Figure 90.16. *Widow,* with bocage. Attributed to Dudson. H: ~10.3". Like the previous figure but with a different base. Price A.

Figure 90.17. *Elijah, Widow,* a pair, with bocages. Attributed to Dudson. H: 11.7" (L), 10.5" (R). The bocages and titling are typical of Dudson. Price A. *Elinor Penna.*

Figure 90.19. Widow and Elijah, a pair, with bocages, with losses. H: 9.2" (L), 11.2" (R). Note the atypical placement of the child to the widow's left and the barrel to her right. Price A. *Northeast Auctions.*

Figure 90.20. Elijah and the widow, a pair, with bocages. H: ~11". Price A.

Figure 90.21. Elijah and the widow, a pair. H: 9". Made without bocages. Several other figures, possibly but not necessarily from the same pot bank, have similarly painted bases. Unusual in that the child is a plump cherub. Price A. *Nicholas Frost Antiques.*

Figure 90.22. Widow, with bocage. H: 10.6". Her dress and eyes are painted with great detail. Perhaps from the same pot bank as the widow in figure 90.20. Price A. *Barbara Gair; www.castle-antiques.com.*

Figure 90.23. Widow, with bocage. Attributed to Dale. H: 10.7". The floral sprigs on the base are specific to Dale. Restored bocage. Price A. *K. Stafford.*

Figure 90.24. *ELIJAH, WIDOW,* a pair, with bocages. H: 11" max. Figures on vermicular bases tend to be finely enameled, and many may originate from the same pot bank. Price B. *Collection of Michael J. Smith.*

Figure 90.25. *ELIJAH,* with bocage. Impressed "WALTON". H: 11". Walton also made this figure with a bocage of large, broad leaves. Companion to the following widow. Price A. *Image courtesy of The Potteries Museum & Art Gallery, Stoke-on-Trent, UK.*

Figure 90.26. *WIDOW,* with bocage. Impressed "WALTON". H: 11.5". Companion to the previous Elijah. Price A. *Peter Flemans.*

Figure 90.28. Widow and Elijah, a pair, with bocages. Attributed to Patriotic Group. H: ~11" max. The holly bocage fronds are specific to the Group. Price B.

Figure 90.27. Widow, with bocage. Attributed to Patriotic Group. H: 10.3". The holly bocage and sprigs on the base are specific to the Group. Price A. *Elinor Penna.*

Figure 90.29. Widow, with bocage. Attributed to Patriotic Group. H: ~10.5". Like the previous two widows but with the cilantro bocage fronds that occur frequently on figures from this Group. Price A.

Figure 90.30. Elijah and the widow, a pair, with bocages. Attributed to Patriotic Group. H: 9.9" (L), 9.7" (R). The bases and bocage leaves and flowers are typical of the Patriotic Group, and the figures are from the same molds used for previous Patriotic Group examples. Price B.

Figure 90.31. Detail of front and reverse of bocage on previous figure of Elijah. Three-leaflet fronds overlap to form an arc, and the large flowers are specific to the Patriotic Group.

Figure 90.32. Widow, with bocage. Attributed to Patriotic Group. H: 10". Made without an oil barrel. Price A. *Peter Flemans.*

Figure 90.33. *ELIJAH* &, with bocage. Attributed to Patriotic Group. H: 9.5". Only the Patriotic Group places titles on small tablets in this manner. Price A. *Peter Flemans.*

Figure 90.34. Elijah, with bocage. Attributed to Patriotic Group. H: ~11". Like the previous figure but untitled and with the pinecone bocage specific to this Group. Price A. *Collection of Michael J. Smith.*

Figure 90.35. Elijah and the widow, with bocages. Attributed to Patriotic Group. H: ~11". Price B.

Figure 90.36. Widow, with bocage. Attributed to Patriotic Group. H: 11". Like the previous widow but painted differently. Price A. *Barbara Gair; www. castle-antiques.com.*

Figure 90.37. Elijah and the widow, a pair, with bocages. The bocages have fern fronds. H: 10.4". Price B. *Guest & Gray Antiques; www. chinese-porcelain-art.com.*

Figure 90.38. Elijah, with bocage. H: 11.5". Like the previous Elijah but with the ordinary five-leaflet bocage fronds with carnations favored by several pot banks. Price A. *Wisbech & Fenland Museum*

Figure 90.39. Widow, with bocage. H: 12.2". Like the previous widow, but the bocage has ordinary five-leaflet fronds with little flowers. Price A. © *Lyon & Turnbull.*

Figure 90.40. Elijah, with bocage. Attributed to Hall. H: ~11". These bocage flowers are characteristic of Hall. They are also on the bocage of a marked Hall Elijah (fig. 90.60). Price A.

Figure 90.41. Widow, with bocage. H: ~10.5". The child, normally on the left, is on the right, and the oil barrel too is on the other side. Price A.

Figure 90.42. & WIDOW, Elijah, a pair, with bocages. Attributed to "Sherratt." H: ~11". The bocages are restored. The sprigs on the mound confirm the attribution, but the painting of her dress and the bases are atypical. Price A.

Figure 90.43. & WIDOW, with bocage. Attributed to "Sherratt." H: ~10". The bocage flowers and the sprigs applied to the base support the attribution. As in the previous example, the "D" in widow is inverted. Price A.

Figure 90.44. Elijah, with bocage. Attributed to "Sherratt." H: 12.6". This base and the applied floral sprigs are specific to "Sherratt." Pairs with the following widow. Price A. *Elinor Penna.*

Figure 90.45. Widow, with bocage. Attributed to "Sherratt." H: 11.7". Pairs with the previous Elijah. Price A. *Elinor Penna.*

Figure 90.46. *ELIJAH*, with bocage. Attributed to "Sherratt." H: ~11.5". Price A.

Figure 90.47. *ELIJAH &, WIDOW*, a pair, with bocages. Attributed to "Sherratt." H: 12" max. The bases, bocages (oak leaves with mayflowers), and applied floral sprigs are specific to "Sherratt." Price B. *Collection of Michael J. Smith.*

Figure 90.48. Elijah, with bocage. Attributed to "Sherratt." H: 11". This rainbow base is not particularly common, and it is one of the prettiest of the "Sherratt" bases. Companion to the next widow. Price B. *Collection of Michael J. Smith.*

Figure 90.49. Widow, with bocage. Attributed to "Sherratt." H: 11". Companion to the previous Elijah. Price B.

Figure 90.50. Elijah, with arch. Attributed to "Sherratt." H: 12". This arch with a cherub atop occurs on other "Sherratt" figures, but in most cases the arch is lost and, at best, only the pillars remain. Pairs with the next widow. Price B.

Figure 90.51. Widow, with arch. Attributed to "Sherratt." H: 12". Arch and columns restored. Pairs with the previous Elijah and, like it, is on a typical "Sherratt" feathered base. Price A.

Figure 90.52. Elijah, with bocage. H: 8.3". An uncommon form. A very similar dress pattern occurs on rare figures of Europa and Liberty and on an unusual figure of Jupiter. Price A. *Kevin Low*

Figure 90.53. Elijah, with bocage. H: ~10". Price A.

Figure 90.54. *WIDOW*, with bocage. Attributed to Box Title Group. H: 9". With losses. Note the turquoise and green base that seems to be specific to Box Title examples. Price A.

Figure 90.55. *WIDOW, ELIJAH*. Attributed to Box Title Group. H: 9" max. With losses. Price A.

Figure 90.56. Elijah, with bocage. H: ~11". Despite the Salt-style bocage, the figure may have been made by any one of several pot banks. Price A.

Figure 90.57. *ELIJAH* (impressed on front edge of base), with bocage. H: ~11". Bocage restored. Note the albino ravens. Price A.

Figure 90.58. *ELIJAH*, with bocage. Attributed to Tunstall Group. H: ~10.5". The bocage flowers exactly match a Tunstall shard, and the fronds are typical of Tunstall.

Figure 90.59. *WIDOW*, with bocage. H: ~9". The child alongside the widow is unusual and is recorded on only this example. Price A.

Figure 90.60. *ELIJAH*, with bocage. Marked "HALL". H. 5.2". Companion to the following widow. Small figures of Elijah and the widow are rarer and more desirable than most large versions. Price A. *Peter Flemans.*

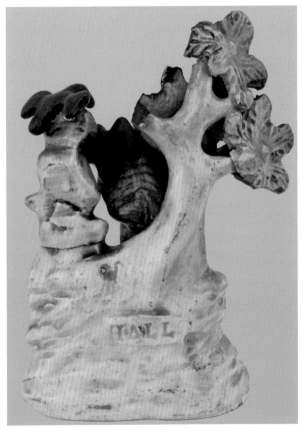

Figure 90.61. *ELIJAH*, reverse of previous figure showing the impressed Hall mark. *Peter Flemans.*

179

Figure 90.62. *WIDOW,* bocage lost. Marked "HALL". H: 4". Companion to the previous Elijah. Price A. *Newcastle-under-Lyme Museum.*

Figure 90.63. *ELIJAH,* with bocage. H: ~5". Companion to the following widow. Price A.

Figure 90.64. *WIDOW,* with bocage. H: ~5.3". Companion to the previous Elijah and, like it, has the Salt-type bocage that multiple pot banks used. Price A. *Collection of Michael J. Smith.*

Figure 90.65. *WIDOW,* with bocage. Attributed to Patriotic Group. H: ~5". The flowers on the bocage are characteristic of the Group. Pairs with the following Elijah. Price A.

Figure 90.66. *ELIJAH*, with bocage. Attributed to Patriotic Group. H: ~5". Pairs with the previous widow. Price A.

Figure 90.67. Widow, with bocage. Possibly made by Dale. H: ~5". The bocage leaves and flowers suggest the attribution.

Figure 90.68. ELIJAH, WIDOW, a pair with bocages. Probably made by Dale. H: 5.3". Some restoration to his bocage. The bocage flowers are consistent with a Dale attribution. Price B. *Woolley and Wallis Salisbury Salerooms Ltd.*

91. Eve

Eve was the first woman, according to *Genesis*. Only one
figure of Eve is recorded.

Figure 90.1. Eve being tempted by the serpent. Height not known.
Price A. *Elinor Penna*.

92. Faith, Hope, Charity

Faith, Hope, and Charity are sometimes called "theological virtues" because Christians believe they are gifts of God. These virtues have traditionally been portrayed in art in female form, each accompanied by an appropriate attribute. Faith holds a book representing the Scriptures. Hope gazes heavenward; the anchor at her side originates from the New Testament, which describes hope as "an anchor of the soul." (Heb. 6:19.) Charity is believed to be the greatest of the virtues, embodying both love of God and others. Appropriately, many figures of Charity portray these dual aspects, with Charity nurturing children, and sometimes one of the children holds a crucifix.

Inexpensive prints applied to glass and detailed hand-colored mezzotints attest to the popularity of the themes of Faith, Hope, and Charity in early nineteenth-century homes. The figures must have been enormously marketable as it seems as if every pot bank produced at least one form.

The figure group of *Roman Charity* is shown among the classical figures in Volume 4, chapter 195.

Figure 92.1. *Faith, Charity, Hope*. Attributed to Ralph Wood. H: 7.5", 8.7", 7.3". Made without bocages. Titling and painting of the bases are typical of Ralph Wood. Faith and Hope are recorded unpainted and impressed "22", but a numbered Charity is not documented. Price B. *www.madelena.com*.

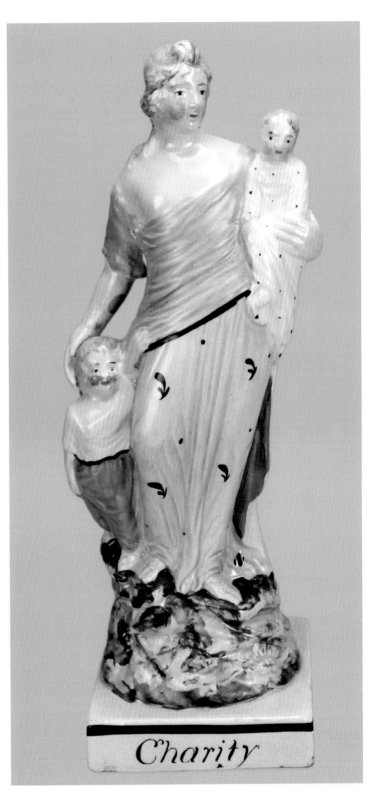

Figure 92.2. *Charity*. Attributed to Ralph Wood. H: 8.8". This form of titling consistently appears on figures that can be attributed to Ralph Wood. Price A.

Figure 92.3. *Charity*. Attributed to Ralph Wood. H: ~8.5". Titled in the same script as the previous figure. The reverse of the base is unpainted. Price A. *Andrew Dando Antiques.*

Figure 92.4. *CHARITY* (impressed on front of base). Impressed "WEDGWOOD". H: 8.6". Price A.

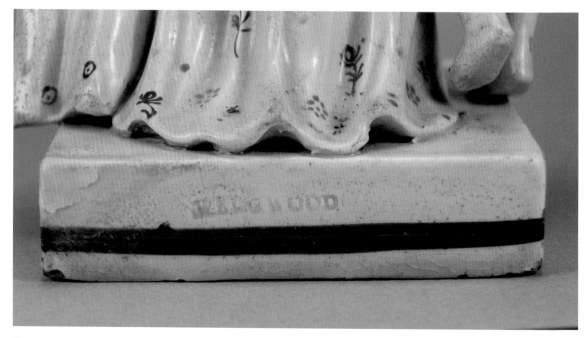

Figure 92.5. The impressed Wedgwood mark on the reverse of the previous figure of Charity.

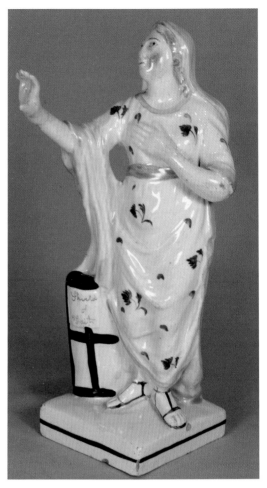

Figure 92.6. Faith. Impressed "WEDGWOOD". H: 7.8". "Shield of Faith" is painted on the shield. A marked Wedgwood figure of Hope is also in the Brighton and Hove Museums. Price A. *Brighton and Hove Museums.*

Figure 92.7. Faith, Charity, Hope, an assembled set. H: 7", 7.2", 6.9". "Sheild of Faith" is painted on Faith's shield. Price A.

Figure 92.8. Faith, Charity, Hope, an assembled set. H: 7", 7.5", 7". Charity and Hope are as in the previous set, but Faith is quite different. Price A.

Figure 92.9. Charity, with bocage. Attributed to Enoch Wood. H: 7.8". Inscribed "T". From excavated Enoch Wood waste wares. *Image courtesy of The Potteries Museum & Art Gallery, Stoke-on-Trent, UK.*

Figure 92.10. Charity, with bocage. Attributed to Enoch Wood. H: 7.2". This figure also occurs impressed "4" or "19" beneath. Closely matches the previous excavated Enoch Wood figure. Companion to the following figures of Hope and Faith. Price A. *Elinor Penna.*

Figure 92.11. Hope, with bocage. Attributed to Enoch Wood. H: 7". This figure also occurs impressed "2" or "19" beneath. Companion to the previous and following figures of Charity and Faith. Bocage restored. Price A. *Elinor Penna.*

Figure 92.13. Faith, Charity, Hope, a set, with bocages. Attributed to "Sherratt." H: 8.5" max. The bocages, bases, dress patterns, and floral sprigs applied to the mounds are typical of "Sherratt." Painted in the turquoise palette "Sherratt" sometimes used. Price B.

Figure 92.12. Faith, with bocage. Attributed to Enoch Wood. H: 7". Companion to the previous figures of Charity and Hope. Occurs impressed "19" beneath. Price A. *Elinor Penna.*

Figure 92.14. Charity, with bocage. Attributed to "Sherratt." H: 8.7". Like Charity in the previous set, but the base and bocage are painted in a different palette. Price A.

Figure 92.15. Charity, with bocage. Attributed to "Sherratt." H: ~8.7". Like previous figures of Charity but with different bocage flowers (mayflowers). Price A.

Figure 92.16. Faith, with bocage. Attributed to "Sherratt." H: 7.5". A companion to Charity in figure 92.14, having the same bocage and base. Price A. *Peter Flemans.*

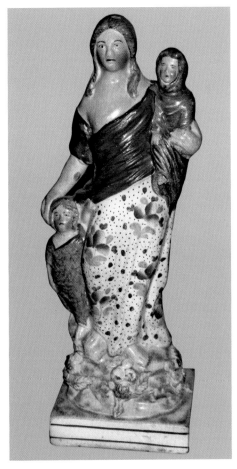

Figure 92.17. Hope, with bocage. Attributed to "Sherratt." H: ~7.7". The typical "Sherratt" bocage differs from the bocages on previous "Sherratt" figures. Price A.

Figure 92.18. Charity. Attributed to "Sherratt." H: ~8.5". Like previous "Sherratt" figures of Charity but made without a bocage. The pink luster on the infant's clothing is a typical "Sherratt" touch. Price A.

187

Figure 92.19. Faith, Charity, Hope, a set. Attributed to "Sherratt." H: 8.5" max. Made without bocages. Floral sprigs on the bases establish the attribution. These bases also occur on "Sherratt" figures of Pomona and Flora. Price B. *Andrew Dando Antiques.*

Figure 92.20. Faith, Charity, Hope, reverse of previous set. *Andrew Dando Antiques.*

Figure 92.21. Hope. Attributed to "Sherratt." H: 8". Like Hope in the previous set but with a typical "Sherratt" dress pattern. Price A. *Collection of Michael J. Smith.*

Figure 92.22. Hope. Attributed to "Sherratt." H: ~7". The mound has characteristic floral sprigs applied to it. A companion to the following Faith. Made without bocage. Price A.

Figure 92.23. Faith. Attributed to "Sherratt." H: ~7". A companion to the previous figure of Hope. Made without bocage. Price A.

Figure 92.24. Faith, Charity, Hope, a set, with bocages. Attributed to "Sherratt." H: ~5.5" max. These bases and bocages occur on many smaller "Sherratt" figures. Price B.

Figure 92.25. *Faith, Charity, Hope,* a set. Probably made by Dudson. H: 7.2", 9", 7". The way the bases are made and painted and the script used for titling suggest the attribution. Price B. *Elinor Penna.*

Figure 92.26. *Faith, Charity, Hope,* a set. H: ~8.5" max. Like the previous set but the script differs from that used by Dudson. A similar example of Hope mistitled *Faith* is recorded. Price B. *Andrew Dando Antiques.*

Figure 92.27. *charity.* Possibly made by Dudson. H: ~8.5". Like the Charity in figure 92.25, and the script suggests the Dudson attribution. Price A.

Figure 92.28. *Charity.* Possibly made by Dudson. H: 8.7". Titled and modeled like the previous example. Cross restored. Price A. *www.madelena.com.*

Figure 92.29. *CHARITY.* H: 8.6". Price A.

Figure 92.30. Charity. H: ~8.5". From the same molds as "Sherratt" figures of Charity, but the floral sprigs on the base are not associated with "Sherratt." Price A.

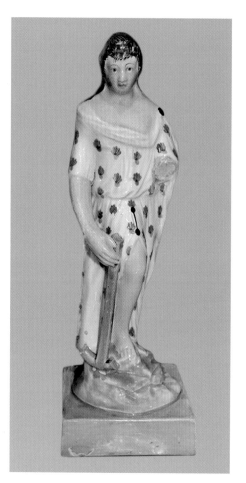

Figure 92.31. Hope. Attributed to Gray Base Group. H: 8.8". Price A.

Figure 92.32. Hope. H: 6.9". Price A. *Nicholas Frost Antiques.*

Figure 92.33. Charity. H: 8.9". Feldspathic ironstone body. Possibly an experimental figure by Chetham & Woolley. No other figure from these molds is recorded. Price B. *Eileen and Robert Carde.*

Figure 92.34. Charity, reverse of previous figure. From beneath, the base has rounded internal corners. *Eileen and Robert Carde.*

Figure 92.35. Faith. H: ~7". Price A. *www.madelena.com.*

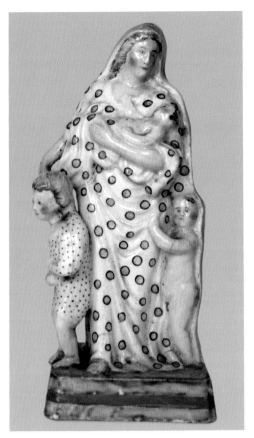

Figure 92.36. Charity. H: ~9". The body is porcelaneous. Price A.

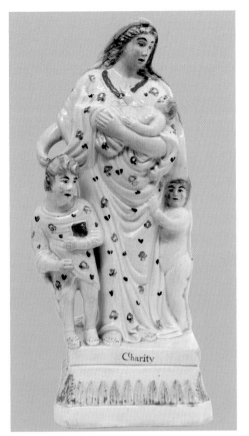

Figure 92.37. *Charity*. Impressed "T. Smith". H: 9.7". The titling uses script otherwise only recorded on Ralph Wood figures. Price A. *Image courtesy of The Potteries Museum & Art Gallery, Stoke-on-Trent, UK.*

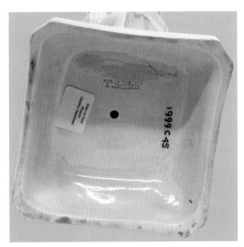

Figure 92.38. Base of the previous *Charity* showing the impressed "T. Smith" mark. *Image courtesy of The Potteries Museum & Art Gallery, Stoke-on-Trent, UK.*

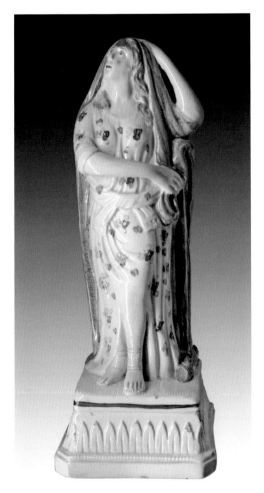

Figure 92.39. Hope. Impressed "T. Smith". H: 9". Price A. *Image courtesy of The Potteries Museum & Art Gallery, Stoke-on-Trent, UK.*

Figure 92.40. Faith, Charity, Hope. H: 8.1", 9", 8.3". Decorated with pink luster. Price C. *John Howard; www.antiquepottery.co.uk.*

Figure 92.41. Faith, Charity, Hope. Reverse of previous set. *John Howard; www.antiquepottery.co.uk.*

Figure 92.42. Hope. H: 9". Price A. *Iconic Design, Edinburgh.*

Figure 92.43. Detail of the unusual large flowers on the base of the previous figure of Hope. *Iconic Design, Edinburgh.*

Figure 92.44. Faith. Impressed "WALTON". H: ~7.5". Uses the same molds as the Walton figure of the Lost Coin. Bocage restored. Price A.

Figure 92.45. Charity. H: ~9". Price A. *John Howard; www.antiquepottery.co.uk.*

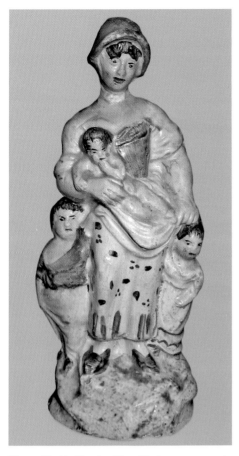

Figure 92.46. Charity. H: ~8". A very unusual model. Price A.

Figure 92.47. Charity. H: 7.2". Price A. *Collection of Arnold and Barbara Berlin.*

Figure 92.48. Charity. H. 8.5". Like the following figure, but the child on the left is quite different. Price A.

Figure 92.49. Charity. H: 8.5". Like previous and following examples, but the child on the left differs. Price A.

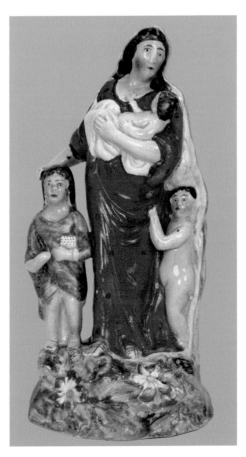

Figure 92.50. Charity. Attributed to Leather Leaf Group. H: 8.3". The two large flowers on the base confirm the attribution. Price A.

Figure 92.51. Charity. Attributed to Leather Leaf Group. H: 8.3". The distinctive large and small flowers on the base establish the attribution. Price A.

Figure 92.52. Hope. H: ~8". Price A.
Andrew Dando Antiques.

Figure 92.53. Hope. H: ~8". Price A.

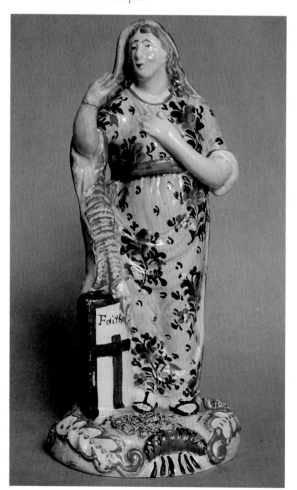

Figure 92.54. *Faith* (painted on shield). H: ~8". Price A.
Aurea Carter Antiques

Figure 92.55. *FAITH* (impressed on shield). Probably made by one of the Scottish potteries. H: 8.7". Hope and Charity are also recorded on this base. Price A. *K. Stafford.*

194

93. The Flight to Egypt and the Return from Egypt

For centuries, artists have depicted Joseph, Mary, and Jesus's Flight to Egypt and Return from Egypt as mirror images. The Return is shown on the eighth century Ruthwell Cross, and in the twelfth century the St. Alban's Psalter portrayed both scenes. By the 1800s, they were depicted in cheap wood cuts on penny broadsides and chapbooks, as well as in crudely colored cottage prints.

The Flight and Return must have been commercially successful figure models in the early 1800s, because several potters fashioned them. Despite their popularity in their time, today it is difficult to find an attractive pair in good condition, but either one stands well on its own. The Flight includes an infant Jesus, while the Return depicts Jesus as a larger child. In most cases, the Flight faces left and the Return faces right. This means that the donkeys stand tail to tail if the Flight is placed to the left, as might be expected for titled pairs. Either group is usually about 7" to 9.5" tall, including bocage. However, one pot bank made larger versions that stand around 9.5" to 10.5", and these were made without bocages. These larger examples stand with the Flight facing right, and the Return facing left (figs. 93.26–27).

Figure 93.1. *RETORN FROM EGYPT, FLIGHT EGYPT*, a pair, with bocages. Impressed "WALTON". H: ~8". The bocage flowers differ from those on the following Walton pair. Price C. *John Howard; www. antiquepottery.co.uk*

Figure 93.2. *RETURN FROM EGYPT, FLIGHT TO EGYPT*, a pair, with bocages. Impressed "WALTON". H: 8.1" (L), 7.7" (R). The Return has cross-shaped bocage flowers; the Flight has six-petalled flowers. Price C. *Collection of Arnold and Barbara Berlin.*

Figure 93.3. *RETURN FROM EGYPT*, with bocage. Impressed "WALTON". H: 8.1". Bocage fronds with large, broad leaves occur infrequently on Walton figures. The bocage flowers are like those on the previous Walton Return but much larger. Price B.

Figure 93.4. *RETURN FROM EGYPT, FLIGHT TO EGYPT*, a pair, with spill vases. Impressed "WALTON". H: 7.9". Price C. *John Howard; www. antiquepottery.co.uk.*

Figure 93.5. Flight to Egypt/Return from Egypt, with bocage. H: ~7". A Salt-type bocage, but no features support attribution. Price A.

Figure 93.6. Return from Egypt, Flight to Egypt, a pair, with bocages. H: 7". Similar to the previous example but painted differently. Also occurs with yellow enamel in place of the pink on the base. Note that the child is the same in both groups, and the groups are mirror images. Price B.

Figure 93.7. Flight to Egypt, with bocage. H: 6". Like the left hand figure in the previous example, but here the child is an infant in arms. Price A. *Michael Goodacre.*

Figure 93.8. Flight to Egypt, with bocage. H: ~7". A mirror-image of the previous example and on a base of the same form. Price A.

Figure 93.9. Flight to Egypt, with bocage. H: 7.5". The infant suggests this is a Flight rather than a Return, even though the donkey faces to the right. Price A. *Brighton and Hove Museums.*

Figure 93.10. Return from Egypt, with bocage. H: ~7.5". On the same base as the previous example and with the same distinctive flower clump on it. The child is larger, so this is probably intended to be a Return rather than a Flight. Price A.

Figure 93.11. Return from Egypt. H: ~7". Made without bocage. On the same base as the previous example and apparently uses the same figure molds (with the child placed differently). Possibly both are from the same pot bank. Price A.

Figure 93.12. Return from Egypt, with bocage. H: 8". An uncommon example with a very large child and an unusual donkey's head. Price A. *Peter Flemans.*

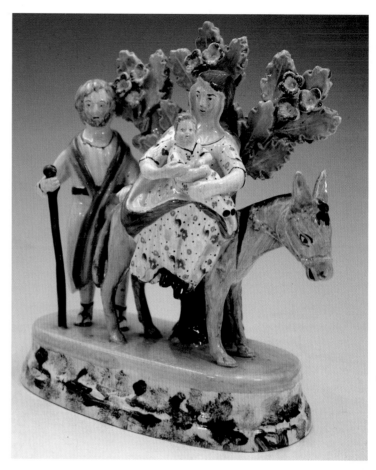

Figure 93.13. Return from Egypt, with bocage. Attributed to "Sherratt." H: ~7.5". The base and bocage are characteristic of "Sherratt." Price B. *John Howard; www.antiquepottery.co.uk.*

Figure 93.14. Return from Egypt, with bocage. Attributed to "Sherratt." H: 7.6". Like the previous example but painted differently. Price B. *Elinor Penna.*

Figure 93.15. Return from Egypt, Flight to Egypt, a pair, with bocages. Attributed to "Sherratt." H: 8". On feathered bases that are specific to "Sherratt." Price C. *Collection of Michael J. Smith.*

Figure 93.16. Return from Egypt, with bocage. Attributed to "Sherratt." H: 8". A less common "Sherratt" base. Price B. *Collection of Michael J. Smith.*

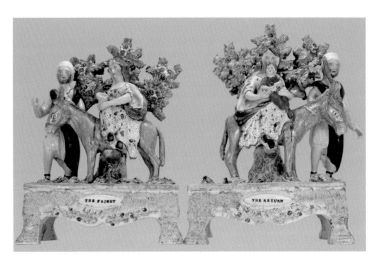

Figure 93.17. *THE FLIGHT, THE RETURN,* a pair, with bocages. Attributed to "Sherratt." H: ~8". Price C.

Figure 93.18. Return from Egypt, with bocage. Attributed to "Sherratt." H: 8.5", L: 6". Like "Sherratt" Return groups in figures 93.16–17, but Joseph now stands behind the donkey, as in figures 93.14–15. Pairs with the following Flight. Price C, pair. *The William Herbert and Nancy Hunt Collection.*

Figure 93.19. Flight to Egypt, with bocage. Attributed to "Sherratt." H: 8", L: 6". Pairs with the previous Return. Price C, pair. *The William Herbert and Nancy Hunt Collection.*

Figure 93.20. *RETURN, FLIGHT &*, with bocages. Attributed to Patriotic Group. H: 9.1". The donkeys must stand tail to tail for the titles to flow correctly. The baby wears a halo in the Flight, and an older child stands on the base of the Return. Price C. *Image courtesy of The Potteries Museum & Art Gallery, Stoke-on-Trent, UK.*

Figure 93.21. *FLIGHT &*, with bocage. Attributed to Patriotic Group. H: ~9". The bocage, base, and title tablet are typical of the Group. Titles on small tablets occur only on Patriotic Group examples. Price B.

Figure 93.22. *FLIGHT &*, with bocage. Attributed to Patriotic Group. H: ~9". Like the previous examples but with a different typical bocage (cilantro leaves) and with characteristic sprigs on the base. Price B. *Andrew Dando Antiques.*

Figure 93.23. Return from Egypt, with bocage. H: ~8". Bases with shield motifs occur most commonly on Flight and Return examples. This base style is also recorded on medium-sized lions (Vol. 3, fig. 126.39) and on one other group (Vol. 4, fig. 199.25), all probably from the same pot bank. Price B. *Andrew Dando Antiques.*

Figure 93.25. Flight to Egypt, Return from Egypt, a pair, with bocages. H: ~7". Bocages restored with one original frond on the Flight. Price A.

Figure 93.24. Flight to Egypt, with bocage. H: ~8". Bocage restored. Companion to the previous example. Price A.

Figure 93.27. Flight to Egypt. H: 9.5". Like the previous Flight but decorated differently. Price B. *Skinner, Inc.; www. skinner.com.*

Figure 93.26. Flight to Egypt, Return from Egypt, a pair. H: 10.5" (L), 9.5" (R). Made without bocages. Here the Flight faces right, and the Return left. Taller than all previous examples, and the figures are larger. Price C. *John Howard; www.antiquepottery.co.uk.*

94. Jeremiah

In the Old Testament *Book of Jeremiah*, written between 630 and 580 B.C.E., Jeremiah warns the people of Israel of oncoming destruction if they do not mend their ways. Figures of Jeremiah are all attributed to the Patriotic Group. The plinth beside Jeremiah is impressed "SCRIPTURES PRESERVED JEREMIAH CH 34". Jeremiah's raised arm is almost inevitably restored or damaged.

Figure 94.2. Jeremiah. Attributed to Patriotic Group. H: 10.7". Like the previous figure but with the large bocage flowers that are specific to this Group. Price B.

Figure 94.1. Jeremiah. Attributed to Patriotic Group. H: 10.4". Price B. *John Howard; www. antiquepottery.co.uk.*

Figure 94.3. Jeremiah. Attributed to Patriotic Group. H: ~10.5". Price B.

Figure 94.4. Jeremiah. Attributed to Patriotic Group. H: 9.9". This low base is less common than the taller base on the previous figures. The holly bocage and sprigs on the base are characteristic of the Patriotic Group. Price B. *Richard F. Deloache, Dallas, Texas.*

95. King David

King David (1040–970 B.C.E.) ruled over the Kingdom of Israel, and the *Book of Samuel* chronicles his reign. All recorded figures of King David are of the same form and all are attributed to Ralph Wood. The figures occur both titled and untitled. They may be unnumbered, or they may be impressed either "28" or "29".

Figure 95.1. *King David.* Attributed to Ralph Wood; impressed "29". H: 12.4". Note the gilding on the base. Price B. *Image courtesy of The Potteries Museum & Art Gallery, Stoke-on-Trent, UK.*

Figure 95.2. *King David*, reverse of previous figure. The number "29" is impressed on the back of the plinth, which is unpainted, as is typical of Ralph Wood figures. *Image courtesy of The Potteries Museum & Art Gallery, Stoke-on-Trent, UK.*

Figure 95.3. *King David.* Attributed to Ralph Wood. H: ~12.3". The portrait medallion on the front of the plinth differs from that on the previous figure. Price B. *Andrew Dando Antiques.*

Figure 95.4. King David. Attributed to Ralph Wood. H: 12.4". Like the previous two figures but lacking a title. The unpainted portrait medallion on the plinth is quite different from those on the previous two figures. Price B. *Brighton and Hove Museums.*

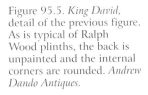 

Figure 95.5. *King David,* detail of the previous figure. As is typical of Ralph Wood plinths, the back is unpainted and the internal corners are rounded. *Andrew Dando Antiques.*

96. Parable of the Lost Coin

The Parable of the Lost Coin (*Luke* 15:8–10) tells of a poor woman who finds a coin she has lost. The parable is one of redemption, with the coin symbolizing a redeemed sinner. Figures portraying this parable can pair with figures depicting the Parable of the Lost Sheep, but the figures were probably not necessarily paired at manufacture and seldom occur in pairs today.

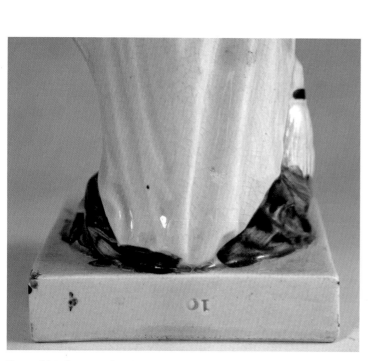

Figure 96.2. *Lost piece found*, reverse of previous figure showing the "10" impressed upside down. *Martyn Edgell Antiques Ltd.*

Figure 96.1. *Lost piece found*. Made by Ralph Wood; impressed "10". H: 10". As on all Ralph Wood figures with similar bases, the painted line bands only three sides of the base. Price B. *Martyn Edgell Antiques Ltd.*

Figure 96.3. *Lost peice found.* Made by Ralph Wood and impressed "W". H: 8.6". Price B. *Aurea Carter Antiques.*

Figure 96.4. Lost Piece Found. Impressed "WEDGWOOD". H: 8.3". Pairs with a Lost Sheep, also made by Wedgwood. Price A.

Figure 96.5. Lost Piece Found, reverse of previous figure, impressed "WEDGWOOD" on the back of the base.

Figure 96.6. *Lost Piece.* Probably made by Dudson. H: ~8". The titling is typical of Dudson. Pairs with a companion *Lost Sheep.* Price A. *Robert Hawker.*

Figure 96.7. Lost Piece Found. H: 9.2". Price A. *Brighton and Hove Museums.*

Figure 96.8. Lost Piece Found. H: 9.2". Like the previous figure, but the base is lacking. Despite this, their heights are the same because of different shrinkage rates in firing. Price A. *Image courtesy of The Potteries Museum & Art Gallery, Stoke-on-Trent, UK.*

Figure 96.9. Lost Piece Found, with bocage. Attributed to Patriotic Group. H: 8.3". This holly bocage only occurs on Patriotic Group figures. Pairs with a companion Lost Sheep. Price B. *Andrew Dando Antiques.*

Figure 96.10. Lost Piece Found, with bocage. Attributed to Patriotic Group. H: 8.3". These distinctive bocage flowers are specific to this Group. Pairs with a companion Lost Sheep. Price B. *Saffron Walden Museum.*

Figure 96.11. Lost Piece Found, with bocage. Impressed "WALTON". From the same molds used for the Walton figure of Faith. H: 7.5". Price B. *Collection of Michael J. Smith.*

Figure 96.12. Lost Piece Found. H: 6". Pairs with a small companion Lost Sheep. Price A.

Figure 96.13. Lost Piece Found and Lost Coin, with bocage. H: 8.5". Known from only this example. From the same pot bank as Volume 4, figure 141.1 (two figures of Old Age on this base and with this bocage). Price B. *Collection of Michael J. Smith.*

97. Parable of the Lost Sheep

The Parable of the Lost Sheep (*Luke* 15:3–7 and *Matthew* 18:12–14) tells of a shepherd who searches for a sheep that is lost. It is a parable of redemption, with the sheep representing a lost human being. Figures portraying the Parable of the Lost Sheep often pair with figures portraying the Parable of the Lost Coin (or Lost Piece), but in all probability the figures were not necessarily sold in pairs.

A figure portraying the Parable of the Lost Sheep impressed "WALTON" remains elusive, although several Walton figures portraying the Parable of the Lost Coin have been documented. On the other hand, a significant number of figures of the Parable of the Lost Sheep apparently lack a companion Parable of the Lost Coin, suggesting that all manufactories did not make both models.

Figure 97.1. *Lost Sheep found, Lost Peice found.* Attributed to Ralph Wood. H: 8.7" (L), 9" (R). Made without bocages. The titling and rainbow palette on the mounds are typical of Ralph Wood figures. Price B. *Andrew Dando Antiques.*

Figure 97.2. *Lost Sheep Found.* Made by Ralph Wood and impressed "W". H: ~8.7". The impressed "W" is visible on the back of the base, as is typical of this mark. The "Ra. Wood Burslem" mark is usually beneath bases. Price B. *Andrew Dando Antiques.*

207

Figure 97.3. Lost Sheep Found. Impressed "9 Ra. Wood Burslem". H: ~8.7". Note that both Ralph Wood's mark and the model number are impressed beneath. Price B.

Figure 97.4. *Lost sheep found.* Attributed to Ralph Wood; impressed "9". H: 8.7". The low number in Ralph Wood's 170-number sequence suggests that this was one of his earlier figure models. Price B. *The William Herbert and Nancy Hunt Collection.*

Figure 97.5. *Lost sheep found,* reverse of previous figure. The "9" is impressed on the center of the base. *The William Herbert and Nancy Hunt Collection.*

Figure 97.6. Lost Sheep Found. Attributed to Ralph Wood; impressed "9". H: 8.3". Like previous figures but untitled. The line bands three sides of the base only. Price A.

Figure 97.7. Lost Sheep Found. Impressed "WEDGWOOD". H: 8.2". Made without bocage. Apparently from the same figure molds as the Ralph Wood figures. Pairs with a Lost Coin also marked "WEDGWOOD". Price A.

Figure 97.8. Lost Sheep Found, reverse of previous figure, impressed "WEDGWOOD" on the back of the base.

Figure 97.9. *Lost Sheep.* Probably made by Dudson. H: 8.9". The titling and the modeling of the base are typical of Dudson. Price A. *Brighton and Hove Museums.*

Figure 97.10. Lost Sheep Found. H: ~8". Price A. *Andrew Dando Antiques.*

Figure 97.11. Lost Sheep Found. Probably made by Enoch Wood. H: 9". Made without bocage. This base occurs routinely on figures attributable to Enoch Wood. Price A. *Nick Burton.*

Figure 97.12. Lost Sheep Found, with dog, with bocage. Probably made by Enoch Wood. H: ~8". Both the base and fern-leaflet bocage fronds are typical of Enoch Wood. Price B. *John Howard; www.antiquepottery.co.uk.*

Figure 97.13. Lost Sheep Found, with dog, with bocage. Probably made by Enoch Wood. H: ~8". Like the previous example but with hawthorn bocage fronds. Enoch Wood was not alone in using this bocage form. Price B. *Andrew Dando Antiques.*

Figure 97.14. Lost Sheep Found, with bocage. Attributed to Patriotic Group. H: 8.3". The bocage flowers are specific to the Group. Pairs with a figure of the Lost Coin. Price B.

Figure 97.15. Lost Sheep Found. Attributed to Patriotic Group. H: ~8.3". Like the previous figure, but with another typical Patriotic Group bocage leaf and flower combination. Price B. *John Howard; www.antiquepottery.co.uk.*

Figure 97.16. Lost Sheep Found, with bocage. Attributed to Patriotic Group. H: 8.3". Like the previous two figures, but with the holly bocage that is characteristic of the Group. Pairs with a figure of the Lost Coin. Price B. *Nick Burton.*

Figure 97.17. Lost Sheep Found. H: 7.9". Price A. *Elinor Penna.*

Figure 97.18. Lost Sheep Found. Attributed to Leather Leaf Group. H: ~6.8". The base and bocage leaves are typical of the Group. Price A.

Figure 97.19. Lost Sheep Found. H: 6". Price A. *Elinor Penna.*

Figure 97.20. Lost Sheep Found. H: 6". Pairs with a Lost Coin of the same reduced scale. Price A. *Andrew Dando Antiques.*

Figure 97.21. *LOST SHEEP.* H: 5.2". An unusual model and the smallest example of this subject. Bocage restored. Price A. *Michael Goodacre.*

211

98. Parable of the Wise and Foolish Virgins

The Parable of the Ten Virgins (*Matthew* 25: 1–13), also known as the Parable of the Wise and Foolish Virgins, tells of ten virgins awaiting the coming of a bridegroom. Each virgin carries an oil torch. The five wise virgins have sufficient oil for their lamps, but the five foolish virgins have not. Because the foolish virgins have to seek more oil, they are not present when the bridegroom arrives. The Wise Virgin has been represented in imagery for centuries holding her oil light, as does the Staffordshire figure. The figures are surprisingly uncommon and the torch is usually lost. A figure portraying the Foolish Virgin has not been documented.

Figure 98.1. The Wise Virgin. H: 8.8". Price A. *Wisbech & Fenland Museum.*

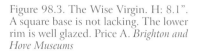

Figure 98.2. The Wise Virgin, reverse of previous figure. *Wisbech & Fenland Museum.*

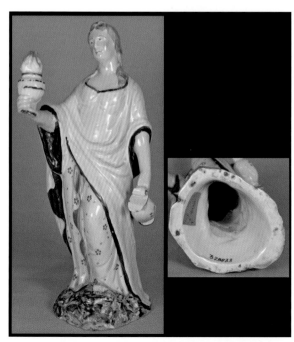

Figure 98.3. The Wise Virgin. H: 8.1". A square base is not lacking. The lower rim is well glazed. Price A. *Brighton and Hove Museums*

99. Sacrifice at Lystra

The New Testament (*Acts* 14:8–18) tells that when Paul and Barnabas visit Lystra, Paul heals a crippled man. The Lystrans believe the two apostles are Greek gods, and, to their horror, bring out bulls to sacrifice to them. Raphael's sixteenth-century cartoon portraying the scene (commissioned for a tapestry for the Sistine Chapel) is the design source for the figure group. A similar Roman relief panel (now in the Louvre) showing similar preparation for the sacrifice at Lystra may have inspired Raphael's work.

This rare group is known from three very similar examples attributable to John Dale. In all cases, the bocage was made separately to fit into a socket, in the manner in which a candle fits into a candlestick. In the example shown, the bocage is lost. Because the group shows the slaughtering of an ox, it is sometimes incorrectly interpreted as portraying the Parable of the Prodigal Son (*Luke* 15:11–32).

Figure 99.1. Engraving of the *Sacrifice at Lystra*, after Raphael.

Figure 99.2. The Sacrifice at Lystra. Four men in classical attire slaughtering an ox, with bocage socket. Attributed to Dale. H: 10.7". This base occurs on other similar groups with definitive Dale characteristics. The figures have facial features typical of Dale. Price B. *Collection of Arnold and Barbara Berlin.*

100. Peter Restoring the Lame Man

In the New Testament, *Acts* Ch. 3, Peter finds a crippled beggar at the Temple gates and restores his ability to walk. Raphael's sixteenth century cartoon (commissioned for a Sistine Chapel tapestry) portrays the scene, and a derivative print probably assisted with designing figure groups depicting this miracle. The groups were made in two styles. Examples on oblong bases occur with or without bocages, while examples on table bases never have bocages. Companion groups of Samuel anointing David were made in these same styles.

Figure 100.1. *PETER RESTORING THE LAME MAN*, with bocage. H: 7.4". Attributed to Box Title Group. Box Title Group bocages often comprise spindly branches with a single frond attached to each. Price B. *Elinor Penna.*

Figure 100.2. *PETTER RISING THE LAME MAN ACTS CH 3.* H: 10.6". Made without bocage. Price B. *Collection of Arnold and Barbara Berlin.*

Figure 100.3. *PETER RESTORING THE LAME MAN*, with bocage. H: 6.6". Decorated in the style of Blue Group, but there is insufficient evidence for attribution. Price B.

Figure 100.4. *PETER RESTORING THE LAME MAN*. H: ~6.5". Made without bocage. Price B.

Figure 100.5. *PETER RESTORING THE LAME MAN*. H: ~6.5". Made without bocage. Price B.

215

101. Raising of Lazarus

The New Testament's *Gospel of John* tells of Jesus visiting Lazarus's sisters, Mary and Martha, four days after Lazarus's death. Moved by the sisters' sorrow, Jesus goes to Lazarus's tomb and prays for Lazarus to come out. Lazarus emerges, wrapped with linen burial bandages. The subject has been popular in art for centuries, and a derivative engraving probably inspired the rare earthenware groups. Only a handful of examples have been documented. All are in the same style, portraying the tale dramatically and rather comically. Major losses to important elements are common. The tombstone (frequently lost or restored) reads "X1 CHAP OF JOHN & 43 VERSE & JESUS CRIED WITH A LOUD VOICE LAZARUS COME FORTH".

Figure 101.1. The raising of Lazarus. Jesus, Lazarus, Mary, and Martha, with bocage. H: 7.5". The exposed positioning of the figures and tombstone on these groups makes them particularly vulnerable, but here all are original. Price C.

Figure 101.2. The raising of Lazarus, detail of previous example. The cup-like bocage flowers are known from only this example. The interior of the base is painted, a feature not documented on any other figure group.

Figure 101.3. The raising of Lazarus. Jesus, Lazarus, Mary, and Martha, with bocage. H: 7.5". Price B. *Image courtesy of The Potteries Museum & Art Gallery, Stoke-on-Trent, UK.*

Figure 101.4. The raising of Lazarus. Jesus, Lazarus, Mary, and Martha, with bocage. Attributed to Patriotic Group. H: ~7.4". The bocage flowers are specific to the Group. Price B.

Figure 101.5. The raising of Lazarus. Jesus, Lazarus, Mary, and Martha, with bocage. H: 8.5". Price C. On the same base as previous examples, but feet have not been cut. Bocage replaced. Price B. *The William Herbert and Nancy Hunt Collection.*

102. Saints Andrew, Philip, Emanuel, Lucy, Sebastian, Barbara, and John the Baptist

Figures of Saints Matthew, Mark, Luke, and John are fairly common, but figures of other saints are far more difficult to find. Among these are saints titled in a manner suggesting they were made for the continental Catholic market. Several of these saints can be attributed to Enoch Wood because they match Enoch Wood figures that were excavated from the Burslem Old Town Hall site in 1938. Among the excavated figures is an unpainted figure of Saint Sebastian, impressed *S. SEBASTIO O. M.* (*São Sebastian Obiit Martyris*). The Kent factory made figures of exactly this form in the early 1900s, and examples marked "E WOOD" and "ENOCH WOOD" can be found for sale, masquerading as earlier figures. It has not been possible to verify the existence of a genuine pre-Victorian enamel-painted Saint Sebastian.

Figure 102.1. *St. Andrew.* Attributed to Ralph Wood; impressed "122". H: 15". Saint Andrew was Jesus's disciple, and his attribute is the x-shaped cross on which he was martyred. Price B. *Image courtesy of The Potteries Museum & Art Gallery, Stoke-on-Trent, UK.*

Figure 102.2. *St. Andrew*, reverse of previous figure. The number "122" is impressed on the bottom edge of the pedestal. *Image courtesy of The Potteries Museum & Art Gallery, Stoke-on-Trent, UK.*

Figure 102.3. *St. Andrew.* Attributed to Ralph Wood. H: 14.7". Like the previous figure but without a number. Price B. *Andrew Dando Antiques.*

Figure 102.4. *St. Phillip.* Attributed to Ralph Wood; impressed "119". H: 14.3". This apostle is known for his preaching in Greece, Syria, and Turkey. Price B. *Brighton and Hove Museums.*

Figure 102.5. *St. Philip.* Attributed to Ralph Wood. H: 14.2". Like the previous figure but with particularly attractive enameling and lacking an impressed number. Price B. *Aurea Carter Antiques.*

Figure 102.6. *St PhilliP.* Attributed to Ralph Wood. H: ~14.5". Plinth bases on Ralph Wood figures are sometimes painted to simulate marble. The formation of the base and the titling support the attribution. Price B. *Andrew Dando Antiques.*

Figure 102.7. *St. PHILIP.* Attributed to Ralph Wood. H: 14.4". Titled in the uppercase script that sometimes occurs on Ralph Wood figures and from the same molds as the previous examples. The letter "P" is painted beneath. Price B. *Image courtesy of The Potteries Museum & Art Gallery, Stoke-on-Trent, UK.*

Figure 102.8. Detail of the plinth base of the previous figure. This uppercase script and the interior of the base are consistent with a Ralph Wood attribution. *Image courtesy of The Potteries Museum & Art Gallery, Stoke-on-Trent, UK.*

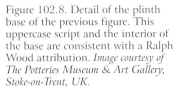

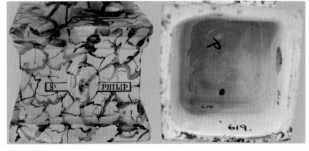

Figure 102.9. *S. MANOEL. M* (St. Emanuel Martyris). Attributed to Enoch Wood; impressed and painted "Nº 5" on the reverse. H: ~8". Figures numbered and styled in this way were among Enoch Wood shards of circa 1825 excavated from the Burslem Old Town Hall site in 1938. Price A.

Figure 102.10. The reverse of the base of the previous figure of St. Emanuel with "Nº 5" impressed and painted.

Figure 102.11. *S. SEBASTI O.M.* (St. Sebastian Obiit Martyris). Attributed to Enoch Wood; impressed "Nº 11" on the reverse. H: 10.4". Excavated from the Burslem Old Town Hall site. Later enamel-painted versions of this figure are commonplace, but an early example has not been documented. *Image courtesy of The Potteries Museum & Art Gallery, Stoke-on-Trent, UK.*

Figure 102.12. *S. LUZIA* (St. Lucy). Attributed to Enoch Wood; impressed and painted "Nº 9" on the reverse. H: 9.1". Saint Lucy (283–204 CE) was a young Christian martyr. A rare figure. Price B. *Elinor Penna.*

Figure 102.13. *S. LUZIA,* reverse of the previous figure showing the impressed "Nº 9".

Figure 102.14. *S. Barbar . V. M.* (St. Barbara Virgin Martyris). Attributed to Enoch Wood; impressed "N⁰ 3" on the reverse. H: 9.4". St. Barbara was a third century virgin martyr. Excavated from the Burslem Old Town Hall site. No enamel-painted version of this figure is known. *Image courtesy of The Potteries Museum & Art Gallery, Stoke-on-Trent, UK.*

Figure 102.15. *S. JOAO* (St. John the Baptist). Attributed to Enoch Wood; impressed and painted "N⁰. 4" on the reverse of the base. H: 9". John the Baptist identified Jesus as the Lamb of God, hence the lamb beside the figure. A rare figure known from only this example. Price B. © *Fitzwilliam Museum, Cambridge.*

Figure 102.16. *S. JOAO,* reverse of the previous figure showing the impressed "N⁰. 4". © *Fitzwilliam Museum, Cambridge.*

103. Saints Matthew, Mark, Luke, and John

The saints have been depicted in art for centuries, and art sources almost certainly inspired earthenware figures of the apostles Matthew, Mark, Luke, and John. Each saint is portrayed with his attribute: Saint Mark with a lion; Saint Matthew with an axe or book or scroll; Saint Luke with an ox; and Saint John with a chalice. Saint John's chalice sometimes has a snake atop. This is because Saint John blessed a cup of poisoned wine, causing the poison to emerge as a snake. These figures can be found in sets of four.

Figure 103.2. *ST LUKE, ST IOHN*, with bocages. H: ~8.2". On the same bases as the previous set. This bocage with these flowers occurs on figure 31.31 and on Volume 3, figure 137.6. Price B.

Figure 103.1. *ST. IOHN, ST MARK, ST LUKE, ST MATTHEW*, with bocages. H: 8". Matthew's raised hand once held a long ax handle, and the ax head is attached to his garment at knee level. Price C. *Brunk Auctions, Asheville, North Carolina.*

Figure 103.3. *S. JOHN*, with bocage. Attributed to "Sherratt." H: 8.3". The bocage establishes the attribution. A companion to the following St. Luke. Price A. *Elinor Penna.*

Figure 103.4. *S. LOKE*, with bocage. Attributed to "Sherratt." H: 8.3". Companion to the previous St. John. Price A.

Figure 103.5. *ST MATTHEW*, with bocage. Attributed to "Sherratt." H: ~ 8". Companion to the previous St. Luke and St. John, but the base is painted differently. Price A.

Figure 103.6. *ST. MARK*, with bocage. Attributed to "Sherratt." H: 7.5". Price A. *Michael Goodacre.*

Figure 103.7. *S LUKE, ST JOHN*, with bocages. Attributed to "Sherratt." H: ~8.1". Bocages restored. Companions to Matthew and Mark in the previous examples. Price A.

Figure 103.8. *ST. MATTHEW*, with bocage. Impressed "WALTON". H: ~7.4". Bocage restored. Forms a set with the following three apostles. Price A.

Figure 103.9. *ST IOHN*, with bocage. Impressed "WALTON". H: ~7.4". Price A.

Figure 103.11. *ST. LUKE*, with bocage. Impressed "WALTON". H: 8". Price A. *Newcastle-under-Lyme Museum.*

Figure 103.12. *ST. LUKE*, reverse of previous figure. *Newcastle-under-Lyme Museum.*

Figure 103.10. *ST MARK*, with bocage. Impressed "WALTON". H: 7.5". Price A. *www.madelena.com.*

Figure 103.13. *ST LUKE*, with bocage. Possibly attributable to Box Title Group. H: ~7.8". Price A.

Figure 103.14. *ST. IOHN*, with bocage. Possibly attributable to Box Title Group. H: 7.5". Price A. *The Bowes Museum, Barnard Castle.*

Figure 103.15. *ST. MARK*, with bocage. H: 8.5". Similar to the following Salt figure but unmarked and probably from some other pot bank. Blue carnations have not been documented on a marked Salt figure. Price A. *Richard F. Deloache, Dallas, Texas.*

Figure 103.16. *ST MARK*, with bocage. Impressed "SALT". H: 9". Price A. *Barbara Gair; www.castle-antiques.com.*

Figure 103.17. *ST. IOHN* (title impressed in base), with bocage. Impressed "SALT". H: ~7.2". Salt apostles occur on the same bases as figures 103.13–14 associated with the Box Title Group. Price A.

Figure 103.18. *ST. IOHN*, with bocage. Impressed "SALT". H: ~8.5". Like the previous figure but with the bocage placed differently. Price A.

Figure 103.19. *ST. MATTHEW* (title impressed in base), with bocage. Impressed "SALT". H: 8.4". Price A. *Barbara Gair; www.castle-antiques.com.*

Figure 103.20. *ST MATTHEW* (title poorly impressed in base) with bocage. Impressed "SALT". H: 8.6". Like the previous figure but with a scroll still present in his left hand. Price A. *The Bowes Museum, Barnard Castle.*

Figure 103.21. *ST LUKE*, with bocage. Impressed "SALT". H: ~9". Price A. *Sam Millar, Grey Abbey Antiques.*

Figure 103.22. *ST. LUKE* (title impressed in base), with bocage. H: 8.7". Like the previous Salt figure but unmarked. Price A. *www.madelena.com.*

Figure 103.23. *ST MATTHEW, ST. MARK, ST LUKE, ST. IOHN*, with bocages. H: 7.5". Indistinguishable from marked Salt figures but unmarked. Price B. *Jonnys Antiques.*

Figure 103.24. *ST. LUKE*, with bocage. H: ~8.1". *ST. MARK* on this base and impressed "HALL" is recorded.[1] Price A. *Brunk Auctions, Asheville, North Carolina.*

Figure 103.25. *ST. LUKE*, with bocage. H: 8.3". Unusual in that the title is on a tablet with canted corners. Price A.

Figure 103.26. *ST. MARK*, with bocage. H: 8.5". The bocage has common carnations, but the base is of a form not seen in previous examples. *ST. MATTHEW* is also recorded on this base. Price A. *The Bowes Museum, Barnard Castle.*

Figure 103.27. *ST. MARK*, with bocage. H: ~8.5". The base appears to be of the same form as the base in the previous example, but the flowers on the bocage (some restoration) are different, as is the painting style. Price A.

Figure 103.28. *ST. IOHN*, with bocage. Attributed to Blue Group. H: ~7.8". The base is like that used by other pot banks, but the distinctive five-petalled flowers on the base and bocage are specific to the Blue Group. A companion to the following figure. Price A.

Figure 103.29. *ST. MATTHEW*, with bocage. Attributed to Blue Group. H: 7.5". A companion to the previous *ST. IOHN*. The flowers support the attribution. Price A. *The Bowes Museum, Barnard Castle.*

Figure 103.30. *ST MATTHEW* (impressed on base), with bocage. Attributed to Blue Group. H: 7". The base is black rather than the typical blue. Note the lavish gilding. The flowers are also gilded, as sometimes seen on Blue Group figures. Price A. *Image courtesy of The Potteries Museum & Art Gallery, Stoke-on-Trent, UK.*

Figure 103.31. *ST. MATTHEW, ST. MARK, ST. LUKE, ST JOHN*, with bocages. Attributed to Blue Group. H: 8.3". With characteristic bocages and painted in the palette that gives the Blue Group its name. Price C. *Bonhams.*

Figure 103.32. *ST MATTHEW*, with bocage.
Attributed to Tunstall Group. H: ~8.5". The
bocage flowers are specific to this Group.
Price A.

Figure 103.33. *ST. MARK*, with bocage.
Attributed to Tunstall Group. H: ~8.5".
Price A.

Figure 103.34. *ST. LUKE*, with bocage. H: ~8.5".
The bocage is restored. The base is like the bases
on the previous two Tunstall figures. Price A.

Figure 103.35. *ST. MATTHEW, ST. MARK, ST. LUKE, ST. IOHN*, a set, with bocages. H: ~8.5" max.
On the same bases as the previous Tunstall examples but exhibiting no specific characteristics. Price C.

Figure 103.36. *ST LUKE*, with bocage. Possibly attributable to Straw Flower Group. H: 7.9". Price A.

Figure 103.37. *ST. MATTHEW, ST LUKE*. H: ~7.5". Made without bocages. Price A.

Figure 103.38. *ST. MARK, ST. IOHN*. H: ~7.5". Made without bocages. The bases are like those used by Salt and several other potters. Price A.

Figure 103.39. *St. John*. Attributed to Ralph Wood. H: 13". Falkner records an example of this figure impressed "120". Price B. *The William Herbert and Nancy Hunt Collection.*

Figure 103.40. St. John. Probably made by Ralph Wood or Enoch Wood/Wood & Caldwell. H: 12.6". *Iohn* is painted within the base. Object lost from hand. Black marbling is documented on Ralph Wood figures but is more suggestive of Enoch Wood/Wood & Caldwell. Price A. *Elinor Penna.*

Figure 103.41. St John, base of previous example with *Iohn* painted within. Figures of Benjamin Franklin, Jupiter, and St. Peter occur on the same base (painted differently), with the title painted within. *Elinor Penna.*

104. Saint Paul

Saint Paul was one of Jesus's apostles. As in art, figures of Saint Paul usually portray him bearded and holding a sword and a book. Saint Paul is often paired with a Saint Peter from the same pot bank.

Figure 104.2. *ST PAUL*, with bocage. Attributed to "Sherratt." H: 10.9". "Sherratt" made *ST PETER* to pair with this figure. Price B. *Elinor Penna.*

Figure 104.1. *St Paul.* Attributed to Ralph Wood. H: 14.3". This figure also occurs impressed "120". Price B. *Image courtesy of The Potteries Museum & Art Gallery, Stoke-on-Trent, UK.*

Figure 104.3. *ST PAUL*. Impressed "WALTON". H: ~9.5". Walton did not make a marked St. Peter to pair with this figure, but many unmarked Walton-style figures of St. Peter are perfect companions. Price A.

Figure 104.4. *SAINT PAUL*, with bocage. Possibly made by Hall. H: ~9". Blue bocage flowers formed and painted like this flower occur on the bocage of a *ST. MARK* with Hall's mark.[1] Price A.

Figure 104.5. *SAINT PETER, SAINT PAUL*, with bocages. Attributed to Blue Group. H: ~9" max. The bocages are specific to the Blue Group. Price B.

Figure 104.6. *SAINT PAUL* (title faintly impressed), with bocage. H: 9". The Salt-type bocage cannot support an attribution. Price A. *Wisbech & Fenland Museum.*

Figure 104.7. *SAINT PAUL* (title faintly impressed) with bocage. H: ~9.2". Restoration to bocage. Price A.

Figure 104.8. *SAINT PAUL*, with bocage. Attributed to Box Title Group. H: 8.6". Price A. *Collection of Michael J. Smith.*

Figure 104.9. *SAINT PAUL*. Attributed to Box Title Group. H: 8.3". Bocage lost. The turquoise and green base is typical of the Group. Price A. *Nick Burton.*

Figure 104.10. *SAINT PAUL*, with bocage. Attributed to Box Title Group. H: 8.7". Price A. *Brunk Auctions, Asheville, North Carolina.*

105. Saint Peter

Saint Peter was one of Jesus's twelve apostles. As in art, Saint Peter is sometimes depicted with keys, a reference to the keys to the kingdom of heaven he received from Jesus. Sometimes he holds a cross; in art this is usually inverted because it is thought that Peter requested to be martyred on an upside-down cross. Figures of Saint Peter typically have a rooster beside the saint. This refers to Jesus saying at the last supper that Peter would deny knowledge of him three times before the rooster next crowed.

Because Saint Peter and Saint Paul are joint patron saints of Rome, pot banks made models of these saints that apparently paired. Interestingly, no example of Saint Peter marked "WALTON" is recorded. However, some unmarked figures of Saint Peter are very much in the Walton style and appear to pair with marked Walton figures of Saint Paul. An example of Saint Peter marked "HALL" is recorded but not shown here.

Figure 105.2. *St Peterus.* Attributed to Ralph Wood. H: 14.5". Price B. *Flinor Penna.*

Figure 105.1. *St Peter.* Attributed to Ralph Wood. H: 14.5". Examples of this figure titled *St. Peter* and *ST. PETRUS* and impressed "117", "118", or "119" (the latter to be added to the list in Vol. 1, Chap 14) are recorded. Price B. © *Fitzwilliam Museum, Cambridge.*

234

Figure 105.3. *St. PETER*. Attributed to Ralph Wood. H: 14.5". St. Philip also occurs on this base, titled similarly. Lacking the crucifix held by previous figures of St. Peter. Price B. *Image courtesy of The Potteries Museum & Art Gallery, Stoke-on-Trent, UK.*

Figure 105.4. Saint Peter. Possibly made by Ralph Wood. H: 14.2". *Peter* is painted within the base. Price B. *Elinor Penna.*

Figure 105.5. Saint Peter, reverse of previous example. *Elinor Penna.*

Figure 105.6. Saint Peter, base of previous example showing *Peter* within. Figures of Benjamin Franklin, St. John, and Jupiter stand on similarly formed plinths with titles painted within. *Elinor Penna.*

Figure 105.7. Saint Peter. Possibly made by Ralph Wood. H: 13.4". Price B. *Andrew Dando Antiques.*

Figure 105.8. *ST PETER*, with bocage. Attributed to "Sherratt." H: 11.4". "Sherratt" made *ST PAUL* to pair with this figure. Price B. *Elinor Penna.*

235

Figure 105.9. *ST PAUL, ST PETER*. Made by Walton (L), attributed to Walton (R). H: 8.3" (L), 9.3" (R). No St. Peter marked Walton is recorded. An unmarked figure can only be attributed when it appears to be in an original pairing with a marked figure. Price B. *Wisbech & Fenland Museum.*

Figure 105.10. *ST PAUL, ST PETER*, reverse of previous pair. The "WALTON" ribbon is integral to the base of St Paul. Walton apparently omitted the ribbon from the mold for St Peter.

Figure 105.11. *ST PETER*, with bocage. Possibly made by Walton. H: ~10". As in the previous example, his book is open to *Luke*. The figure is unmarked and the generic bocage cannot support an attribution. Price B.

Figure 105.12. *ST PETER*, with bocage. Possibly made by Walton. H: 9.9". Like the previous figure. A bocage painted in this manner is recorded on a marked Walton figure, but other pot banks sometimes painted bocages similarly. The book is open to *Luke*. Price A.

Figure 105.13. *ST PETER*, with bocage. Possibly made by Walton. H: 9.9". This is a less-common Walton bocage form, but other potters used it too. The book is open to *John*. The rooster is not original to this figure. Price A.

Figure 105.14. *ST PETER*, with bocage. H: ~10". Very like the three previous figures but with a different bocage, and the book is open to *Mark*. These three-leaflet bocage fronds do not occur on marked Walton figures. Price B. *Elinor Penna.*

Figure 105.15. *ST. PETER*, with bocage. H: ~10". These very large bocage leaves occur on a handful of other fine figures (fig. 63.12, and Vol. 3, fig. 121.1). The book is open to *John*. Price B. *Image courtesy of The Potteries Museum & Art Gallery, Stoke-on-Trent, UK.*

Figure 105.16. *SAINT PETER*, with bocage. Attributed to Blue Group. H: ~9.2". Price A.

Figure 105.17. *SAINT PETER* (title faintly impressed), with bocage. Attributed to Tunstall Group. H: ~10". The bocage (with restoration) and flowers are typical of the Group. Price A.

Figure 105.18. *SAINT PETER*, with bocage. Attributed to Hall. H: ~9". These flowers only occur on a marked Hall Elijah and on figures that link to Hall. Price A.

Figure 105.19. St Peter, with bocage. H: 9.4". Price A. *Barbara Gair; www.castle-antiques.com.*

Figure 105.20. *SAINT PETER* (title very faintly impressed), with bocage. H: 9.2". Price A. *The Bowes Museum, Barnard Castle.*

Figure 105.21. *SAINT PETER*, with bocage. Attributed to Box Title Group. H: ~9.2". Price A.

Figure 105.22. St. Peter. H: 7.7". Made without bocage. A figure emblematic of water with William Absolon's mark is decorated similarly (Vol. 4, fig. 153.10). Price A.

106. Samuel Anointing David

In the Old Testament, *Samuel* 16, God tells Samuel to find a new king to replace Saul. Samuel inspects Jesse's seven sons. He rejects the older six sons, but when David, Jesse's youngest son, comes before him, he anoints him as the next King of Israel.

Figure groups of Samuel anointing David occur in two styles. Examples on oblong mound bases were made with or without bocages, while those on table bases always lack bocages. Figure groups of Peter restoring the lame man were made in these same styles, and the groups were probably intended to be companions.

Figure 106.2. *SAMUEL ANOINTING DAVID*. H: ~7". Made without bocage. Price A.

Figure 106.1. *SAMUEL ANOINTING DAVID*, with bocage. Attributed to Box Title Group. H: 7.1". Price B.

Figure 106.3. *SAMUEL ANOINTING DAVID.* H: ~7". Made without bocage. A different figure of Samuel than in the previous two examples. Price A.

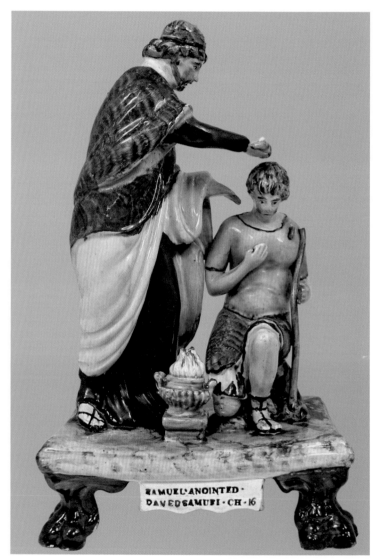

Figure 106.4. *SAMUEL ANOINTED DAVED SAMUEL CH 16.* H: 9.5". Made without bocage. Price B. *Image courtesy of The Potteries Museum & Art Gallery, Stoke-on-Trent, UK.*

Figure 106.5. *SAMUEL ANOINTED DAVED SAMUEL CH 16.* H: ~10". Made without bocage. Price B.

240

107. The Virgin Mary

The Virgin Mary, or Madonna, is the mother of Jesus, and she is traditionally shown holding her infant. The most sophisticated earthenware Madonna and child figure groups portray the Madonna seated, and they are traditionally attributed to Enoch Wood/Wood & Caldwell (figs. 107.1–3). This model is after a circa 1671 fifteen-inch terracotta by the baroque Flemish sculptor, Lucas Fayd'herbe. The terracotta was at Gopsall Hall from 1773 to 1918 and it is currently in the British Museum. Figure groups after the terracotta and on a square base have the Madonna seated on a stool with free-standing rear legs; groups on a rounded base seat the Madonna on a mound. A bronze-glazed example on a rounded base in the Victoria and Albert Museum (C.480–1918) is impressed "WOOD & CALDWELL". Other less refined seated Madonna and child groups are formed similarly and are probably after the Enoch Wood/Wood & Caldwell model.

Madonna and child groups portraying Mary standing rather than seated date from the eighteenth century. The earliest is probably the Ralph Wood model (figs. 107.10–13), and its form seems to have inspired replication. Some of the later groups have inscriptions suggesting that they were made for export to the continental Catholic market. Such religious figures often have holes to accommodate metal fittings.

Figure 107.1. Madonna and child. Probably made by Enoch Wood /Wood & Caldwell. H: 13.3". The stool legs are free-standing. Price C. *John Howard; www. antiquepottery. co.uk.*

Figure 107.2. Madonna and child. Probably made by Enoch Wood /Wood & Caldwell. H: ~13". The stool legs are free-standing, as in the previous example. Price C. *Andrew Dando Antiques.*

Figure 107.3. Madonna and child. Probably made by Enoch Wood /Wood & Caldwell. H: 13". The stool evident in the previous examples has been replaced with a mound. Price C. *Aurea Carter Antiques.*

Figure 107.4. Madonna and child. H: 11.5". Mary sits on a stool. Examples such as this are after the more sophisticated groups previously shown. Price B. *Elinor Penna.*

Figure 107.5. *VIRGIN MARY.* Madonna and child. H: 11". Mary sits on a stool. Price C. *The William Herbert and Nancy Hunt Collection.*

Figure 107.6. Reverse of the previous *VIRGIN MARY.* Note the open well in the base beneath the stool. *The William Herbert and Nancy Hunt Collection.*

Figure 107.7. Madonna and child. H: ~11". Mary is seated on a stool. Price B.

Figure 107.8. *THE VIRGIN MARY.* Madonna and child. Attributed to "Sherratt." H: 11.2". A less common form of the "Sherratt" base. The bocage and floral sprigs on the mound are characteristic of "Sherratt." Price B. *Elinor Penna.*

Figure 107.9. *THE VIRGIN MARY.* Madonna and child. Attributed to "Sherratt." H: ~12.5". Characteristic "Sherratt" base, bocage, and floral sprigs. Also occurs on a marbled table base titled *THE VIRGIN* and *MARY* on two plaques. Price C.

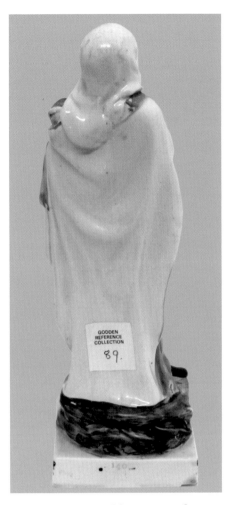

Figure 107.10. *Virgin Mary*. Madonna and child. Attributed to Ralph Wood; impressed "140". H: 9.8". Ralph Wood made some figures in both porcelain and earthenware. This figure is from the same molds as the following porcelaneous figure and is similarly marked. Price A. *Michael Midkiff*.

Figure 107.11. *Virgin Mary*. Madonna and child. Attributed to Ralph Wood; impressed "140". H: 9.1". Very like the previous figure, but the body is porcelaneous. Price A. *Geoffrey Godden Reference Collection, the Potteries Museum*.

Figure 107.12. *Virgin Mary*, reverse of previous figure with "140" impressed on the unpainted back of the base. The earthenware example in figure 107.10 is similarly marked. *Geoffrey Godden Reference Collection, The Potteries Museum*.

Figure 107.16. Base of the previous *Virgin Mary*. The large x-sprigs on the base are specific to Dudson. *The William Herbert and Nancy Hunt Collection*.

Figure 107.13. *Virgin Mary*. Madonna and child. Attributed to Ralph Wood. H: 7.5". This color palette is typical of Ralph Wood figures titled in large black script. Price A.

Figure 107.14. *Virgin Mary*. Madonna and child. Attributed to Dudson. H: 9.5". The x-sprigs on the base are characteristic of Dudson, and Dudson figures are routinely titled in this script. Price A. *Elinor Penna*.

Figure 107.15. *Virgin Mary*. Madonna and child. Attributed to Dudson. H: 9". Dudson favored brown bases. Like the previous figure and with titling in the same script. Price A. *The William Herbert and Nancy Hunt Collection*.

243

Figure 107.17. *SANCTA MARIA, ORA PRO NOBIS* (Holy Mary, Pray for Us). Madonna and child. Probably made by Enoch Wood. H: 23". Intended for the Catholic continental market. Price C. *Andrew Dando Antiques.*

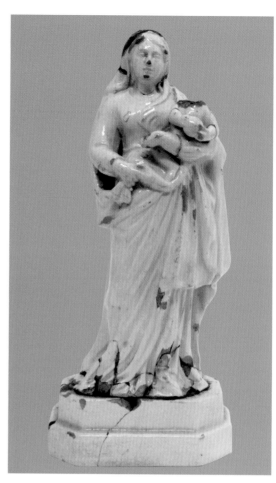

Figure 107.18. Madonna and child. Attributed to Enoch Wood. H: 7.5". Impressed "28". From the Enoch Wood wares of circa 1825 excavated from the Burslem Old Town Hall site. *Image courtesy of The Potteries Museum & Art Gallery, Stoke-on-Trent, UK.*

Figure 107.19. *N. S. DOBOM DESPACHO* (Our Lady of Good Delivery). Madonna and child. Attributed to Enoch Wood. H: 7.7". Like the previous figure. Titled for the Portuguese market. Traces of gilding remain on the skirt. A hole in the head supported a metal crown. Price A. *Brighton and Hove Museums.*

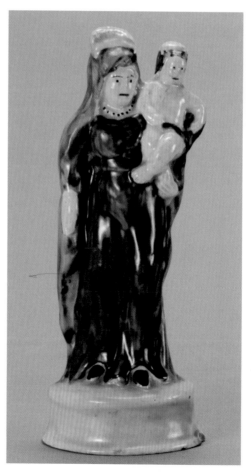

Figure 107.20. Madonna and child. H: 5". Price A.

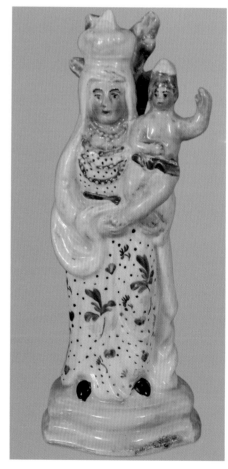

Figure 107.21. Madonna and child, with bocage. H: 5". Price A. *The William Herbert and Nancy Hunt Collection.*

108. The Tithe Pig

A tithe is a payment-in-kind of one-tenth of annual produce. From Norman times, parishioners supported their clerics and funded pastoral care by paying tithes. The close-knit relationship between church and state made tithing to the Church of England mandatory for those of all religious persuasions. Tithing was rife with inequities, and collecting tithes pitted parsons against their resentful communities. The problems seemed too contentious to resolve, but the Great Tithe Act of 1836 took the first step by replacing tithes with a tithe rent charge that remained in place until the Tithe Act of 1936 ended tithing.

In the eighteenth century, England's porcelain factories manufactured figure groups depicting a farmer and his wife offering the parson their tithe produce, including their tenth pig and their tenth child. This humorous scene was based on a mid-eighteenth century engraving by Louis Peter Boitard, and transfer prints of it quickly found their way onto everything from tiles to dinnerware. The design remained relevant into the nineteenth century, and Staffordshire's potters created lively figure groups after Boitard's engraving and earlier Derby groups. The folksy nature of pottery is an ideal medium for capturing the raw humor in this rustic scene.

Not shown in this work is a figure in the Captain Price collection of a vicar impressed "I WILL HAVE NO CHILD THO THE X PIG&C".[1] The base is enameled in a colorful marble pattern not inconsistent with a Ralph Wood attribution. In the same collection are two color-glazed figures of the same form (albeit on different bases) as well as a companion figure of a farmer's wife holding an infant, presumably the tenth child. As yet, no enamel-painted figure of the farmer's wife has been documented.

Figure 108.1. *La Dime. The Tythe Pig*, by Louis Peter Boitard after Müller, circa 1750.

Figure 108.2. Tithe pig group, with bocage. Attributed to Patriotic Group. H: 9". This pinecone bocage is exclusive to the Patriotic Group. Price C. *Andrew Dando Antiques.*

Figure 108.3. *TYTHZ PIG*, with bocage. Attributed to Patriotic Group. H: ~9". Like the previous example but with cilantro bocage fronds. Similar title tablets occur only on figures from this pot bank. Price C.

Figure 108.4. Tithe pig group, with bocage. Attributed to Patriotic Group. H: 8". The base and bocage fronds comprising three hawthorn leaves are consistent with attribution. The mother holds the baby differently than in the previous example. Price B. *John Howard; www.antiquepottery.co.uk.*

Figure 108.5. Tithe pig group, with bocage. Attributed to Patriotic Group. H: ~8". A Patriotic Group base coupled with fern bocage fronds with typically pronounced central veins. Price B.

Figure 108.6. Tithe pig group, with bocage. Attributed to Patriotic Group. H: 8.1". These holly bocage leaves occur only on Patriotic Group examples. They are not normally curled but here have been fashioned in keeping with the look of bocages on porcelain tithe pigs. The fine dress pattern is typical of the Patriotic Group. Price C.

Figure 108.7. Tithe pig group, with bocage. Attributed to Grape Group. H: 8.3". The leaves are curled to mimic the look of porcelain tithe pig groups. Price C.

Figure 108.8. Tithe pig group, with bocage. H: ~7.2". The Salt-type bocage cannot support an attribution. Price B. *John Howard; www. antiquepottery.co.uk.*

Figure 108.9. Tithe pig group, with bocage. H: 7.3". The parson is unusual in that he wears white. Price B. *Collection of Michael J. Smith.*

Figure 108.10. Tithe pig group, with bocage. Probably attributable to Box Title Group. H: ~6.5". Basket handles on tithe pig groups are commonly restored or lost. Price B. *Andrew Dando Antiques.*

Figure 108.11. Tithe pig group, with bocage. Probably attributable to Box Title Group. H: 6.5". Like the previous example but in a brighter palette. Small differences impart great individuality to these groups. Price B. *Peter Flemans.*

Figure 108.12. Tithe pig group, with bocage. H: 7.3". These three-leaflet bocage fronds occur on other figures that form a Group that has not yet been classified. Price B. *Elinor Penna.*

Figure 108.13. Tithe pig, with bocage. H: ~7.5". Like the previous example but with common five-leaflet bocage fronds. Price B.

Figure 108.14. Tithe pig group, with bocage. H: 7.5". This particularly pretty base also occurs on performing bear groups. Price B. *Elinor Penna.*

Figure 108.15. Tithe pig group, with bocage. H: ~ 7.5". Like the previous example but with different bocage flowers, a different basket, and differences in detailing. The two groups may or may not come from the same pot bank. Price B. *Collection of Susan and Richard Cann.*

Figure 108.16. Tithe pig group, reverse of previous example. *Collection of Susan and Richard Cann.*

Figure 108.17. Tithe pig group, with bocage. H: ~7.5". Similar to the previous two examples but with different bocage flowers. These three groups may or may not come from the same pot bank. Price B. *Andrew Dando Antiques.*

Figure 108.18. Tithe pig group, with bocage. Attributed to Leather Leaf Group. H: ~7". Some bocage restoration. The original bocage leaves and flowers support the attribution. Price A.

Figure 108.19. Tithe pig group, with bocage. Attributed to Leather Leaf Group. H: ~7". The bocage leaves and acorns support the attribution. On the same base as the previous group but with the scrolls painted in a typical Leather Leaf Group style. Price B.

Figure 108.20. Tithe pig group, with bocage. Attributed to Leather Leaf Group. H: ~7". The bocage leaves are typical, and these large flowers occur on other Leather Leaf examples. The base is the same as that on the previous two groups. Price B.

Figure 108.21. Tithe pig group, with bocage. Attributed to Leather Leaf Group. H: ~7". The curled bocage leaves, acorns, and base are typical of the Group. Resembles the previous three examples. Restoration to the left side of the bocage. Price A.

Figure 108.22. Tithe pig group, with bocage. H: ~8". The long, droopy bocage leaves emulate the look of the bocage leaves made fashionable on Derby tithe pig groups. Price A.

Figure 108.24. Reverse of bocage on previous tithe pig group. The fronds (with one leaflet atop four others) are typical of Enoch Wood. *Wisbech & Fenland Museum.*

Figure 108.23. Tithe pig group, with bocage. Probably made by Enoch Wood. H: 7". Price A. *Wisbech & Fenland Museum.*

Figure 108.26. Tithe pig group, with bocage. H: ~8". The droopy bocage leaves differ from those on previous examples. Price A.

Figure 108.25. Tithe pig group, with bocage. H: 6.8". The bocage comprises fern-type fronds. Price A. *Image courtesy of The Potteries Museum & Art Gallery, Stoke-on-Trent, UK.*

Figure 108.27. Tithe pig group, with bocage. H: ~8". With the same base and possibly the same bocage leaves as the previous example, and both are probably from the same pot bank. The Leather Leaf Group also uses this base. Price A.

Figure 108.28. Tithe pig group, with bocage. H: ~8". On the same base as the previous two examples but with different bocage leaves. Price A.

Figure 108.29. Tithe pig group, with bocage. Possibly made by Hall. H: ~6.8". This base also occurs on a performing animal group that, like this one, has a bocage with acorns suggestive of a Hall attribution. Price A.

Figure 108.30. Tithe pig group, with bocage. H: ~7". Price B. *Elinor Penna.*

Figure 108.31. Tithe pig group, with bocage. H: ~7". The decoration is unusual. These large twelve-petalled bocage flowers are only otherwise documented on figures 31.31, 103.2, and on Volume 3, figure 137.6. Price B.

Figure 108.32. Tithe pig group, with bocage. H: ~6.8". The base is molded like the base in the previous three examples. The bocage is most unusual. Price B.

Figure 108.33. Detail of the unusual bocage on the previous example.

Figure 108.34. Tithe pig group, with bocage. H: ~8". Restored bocage. Price A.

Figure 108.35. Tithe pig group, with bocage. H. ~7.8". The bocage leaves are unusual. As in many examples, the woman is quite petite. Price A.

Figure 108.36. Tithe pig group, with bocage. H: 6.8". An unusual bocage and, as in the previous example, the woman is small. Price B. *Andrew Dando Antiques.*

Figure 108.37. Reverse of the bocage on the previous tithe pig group. This bocage occurs on a small, unclassified array of figures (for examples see fig. 85.19; Vol. 1, figs. 26.64, 28.43; and Vol. 3, fig. 131.85). *Andrew Dando Antiques.*

Figure 108.38. Tithe pig group, with spill vase. H: 8.5". Tithe pig spill vase groups seem to have identically formed spill vases and bases, but the smaller components and decorative details vary. Price C. *John Howard; www.antiquepottery.co.uk.*

Figure 108.39. Tithe pig group, with spill vase. H: 8.5". With the same major components as the previous example, but the basket is from different molds and decorative details vary. Price C. *Collection of Michael J. Smith.*

Figure 108.40. Tithe pig group, with spill vase. H: 8.5". The unusual parson is only known on this example and as a small free-standing figure (fig. 109.18). Price C. *Richard Montgomery.*

109. Religious Officials and Observers

By the late 1700s, the Church of England's high-living clergy had become ready targets for ridicule, and Staffordshire figure groups mirror this theme. A well-known figure group sometimes titled *Vicar and Moses* portrays a befuddled parson and his clerk, staggering along arm in arm (figs. 109.2–6). Such groups are after one of the woodcut images that illustrated broadsheet ballads titled *The Vicar and Moses*. The ballad's narrative, with words by G.A. Stevens, tells of the clerk, Moses, who comes to the tavern to summon the vicar to bury an infant. Instead, the clerk drinks with the vicar, and both men totter home past midnight.

Another equally well-known group portrays the parson and his clerk in church (figs. 109.8–12). This time, the parson is dozing in the pulpit, while the clerk is earnestly addressing the congregation. The design source for this group is *The Sleeping Congregation*, engraved by William Hogarth and first issued in 1736. Confusingly, this group is also known as *The Vicar and Moses*, but sometimes it is dubbed the *Parson and Clark*. The title *The Vicar and Moses* seems most appropriate because color-glazed examples made by Ralph Wood are impressed thus on the pulpit. Enamel-painted examples attributable to Ralph Wood and impressed "62" and "63" have been documented. However, the examples shown here seem to postdate the Ralph Wood era.

Both Vicar and Moses groups were made into the Victorian era, and it can be difficult to determine their age. Late examples of the Vicar and Moses/Parson and Clerk incised on the back "R. WOOD 1794" occur. Such groups were made some time prior to the 1920s.[1]

Religious officials of varying denominations are shown here. In England, there is no separation of church and state, and the Anglican Church is the nation's church. Being of another religious persuasion was not easy in the pre-Victorian era, and for that reason Catholicism did not have a strong foothold in England. However, a number of figures of Catholic interest were made (figs. 109.23–32). These are believed to have been for the continental Catholic market, and some match Enoch Wood figures excavated from the Burslem Old Town Hall site.

Figure 109.1. *The Vicar and Moses*, published by Carington Bowles, circa 1785. © *Trustees of the British Museum.*

Figure 109.2. *Vicar and Moses.* H: 11.8". Figures of St. George and the dragon as well as Vicar and Moses groups stand on bases formed and titled in the same manner. Price B. *Andrew Dando Antiques.*

Figure 109.3. The Vicar and Moses. H: ~9.5". Made without bocage. Price B. *Andrew Dando Antiques.*

Figure 109.4. The Vicar and Moses. H: ~9.5". Made without bocage. Price B. *Andrew Dando Antiques.*

Figure 109.5. The Vicar and Moses. H: 9". Made without bocage. Price B. *Andrew Dando Antiques.*

Figure 109.6. The Vicar and Moses, with bocage. H: ~9". Unusual to find this group with a bocage. The lantern and base are as on the previous example, and both are probably from the same pot bank. Price B. *Andrew Dando Antiques.*

257

Figure 109.7. *The Sleeping Congregation,* engraved by William Hogarth.

Figure 109.8. The Vicar and Moses. H: 8.9". Price B. *Image courtesy of The Potteries Museum & Art Gallery, Stoke-on-Trent, UK.*

Figure 109.9. The Vicar and Moses. H: 8". Price B. *Newcastle-under-Lyme Museum.*

Figure 109.10. The Vicar and Moses. H: ~9". Price B. *John Howard; www.antiquepottery.co.uk.*

Figure 109.11. The Vicar and Moses. H: 9".
Price B. *John Howard; www.antiquepottery.co.uk.*

Figure 109.12. The Vicar and Moses.
H: 8.5". Price B. *The Bowes Museum,
Barnard Castle.*

Figure 109.13. Clerk. H: 4.4". Made without bocage.
Pairs with the following figure of a parson. Price A.

Figure 109.14. Parson. H: 4.5". Made without bocage.
Pairs with the previous figure of a clerk. Price A.

Figure 109.15. Vicar, with bocage. H: 3.6". Price A.

Figure 109.16. *VICAR* (impressed in base) with bocage. H: ~3.5". The base and bocage flowers differ from those on the previous figure. With losses. Price A.

Figure 109.17. Parson and clerk, with bocage. H: ~4.8". Price A.

Figure 109.18. Vicar. H: 5". A rare small figure only otherwise recorded on a large tithe pig group (fig. 108.40). Price A. *The William Herbert and Nancy Hunt Collection.*

Figure 109.19. Vicar, reverse of the previous figure. *The William Herbert and Nancy Hunt Collection.*

Figure 109.20. The Reverend John Wesley. H: 8.4". Wesley (1703–1791), an Anglican cleric, founded the Methodist Movement that formally separated from the Anglican Church after his death. Price A. *Martyn Edgell Antiques Ltd.*

Figure 109.21. The Reverend John Wesley. H: 8". Wesley preached in the Potteries in the eighteenth century. He was beloved by its working classes and remained inspirational for decades after his death. Price A. *Northeast Auctions.*

Figure 109.22. The Reverend John Wesley. H: 6.3". The base is very suggestive of "Sherratt." Price A. *Peter Flemans.*

Figure 109.23. Monk or priest. Probably made by Enoch Wood. H: 4.8". Similar to figure 109.25, with variations in the head, the base, and the garment. Price A.

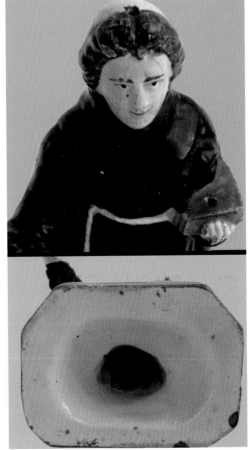

Figure 109.24. Details of the previous figure. A hole atop the head and another atop the prayer book once held metal objects, perhaps a halo and crucifix respectively.

Figure 109.25. Monk or priest. Attributed to Enoch Wood. H: 7.9". Matches the following Enoch Wood figure impressed "24" excavated from the Burslem Old Town Hall site. Unusual in that original gilding is still present. A hole atop the head and another atop the prayer book once held a metal halo and crucifix respectively. Price A. *www.madelena.com.*

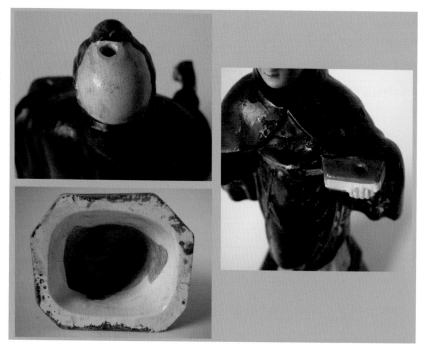

Figure 109.26. Details of the previous figure showing the base and the holes in the head and book. *www. madelena.com.*

Figure 109.27. Monk or priest. Attributed to Enoch Wood. H: 7.5". Excavated from the Burslem Old Town Hall site associated with Enoch Wood. Several similar figures and shards were excavated, some impressed "24". *Image courtesy of The Potteries Museum & Art Gallery, Stoke-on-Trent, UK.*

Figure 109.28. Monk or priest. Attributed to Enoch Wood. H: 10.2". Holes in the head and book accommodate a metal halo and crucifix respectively. Enoch Wood made closely similar figure of monks or priests in two sizes, this being the larger. Figures in both sizes (both impressed "24") were excavated from the Burslem Old Town Hall site. Price A. *Elinor Penna.*

Figure 109.29. Nun holding a laurel branch. Probably made by Enoch Wood. H: 9.9". Price A. *Collection of Arnold and Barbara Berlin.*

Figure 109.30. Nun. Probably made by Enoch Wood. H: 7". Price A. *Collection of Arnold and Barbara Berlin.*

Figure 109.31. Lady in prayer. Probably made by Enoch Wood. H: 7". In the style of other Enoch Wood figures of circa 1825 from the Burslem Old Town Hall site. A snake circles the round mound atop the pedestal. Price A. *Elinor Penna.*

Figure 109.32. Nun. H: 8.5". Probably made for the continental Catholic market. Price A. *Elinor Penna.*

Figure 109.33. Budai Heshang. H: 4". In the 1720s, Meissen made this Laughing Buddha in imitation of Chinese blanc-de-chine figures. Chelsea produced its own "Gross Chinamen" in 1746. After 1750, the Potteries' adaptations catered to the chinoiserie craze. Price A. *Collection of Arnold and Barbara Berlin.*

Figure 109.34. *Worshiper.* Attributed to Ralph Wood; impressed "70". H: 7.4". Price B. *Brighton and Hove Museums.*

Figure 109.35. *Worshiper*. Attributed to Ralph Wood; impressed "69". H: 7.5". Price B. *Image courtesy of The Potteries Museum & Art Gallery, Stoke-on-Trent, UK.*

Figure 109.36. *Worshiper*, reverse of previous example. The number "69" is impressed on the back edge of the base. *Image courtesy of The Potteries Museum & Art Gallery, Stoke-on-Trent, UK.*

Figure 109.37. *Peasant Worshiping*. Attributed to Ralph Wood; impressed "68". H: 7.4". Like the previous two figures but in the brighter palette sometimes found on unnumbered Ralph Wood figures. Price B. *Image courtesy of The Potteries Museum & Art Gallery, Stoke-on-Trent, UK.*

Figure 109.38. *Worshiper*. Attributed to Ralph Wood. H: 7.1". The hat is behind the figure, to the right. Placement of the hat seems to have been quite arbitrary and cannot be linked to impressed numbers or to the lack thereof. Price B. *Collection of Arnold and Barbara Berlin.*

Figure 109.39. Monk. Made by one of the Scottish east coast pot banks. H: 7.3". The box on the monk's lap has a removable lid. Price B.

110. Prepare to Meet Thy God

Large earthenware groups titled *PREPARE TO MEET THY GOD* are attributed to "Sherratt" and are replete with symbols of Masonic significance (figs. 110.1–2). The words "Prepare to meet thy God, O Israel" are from *Amos* 4:12 and are interpreted as a reminder of man's mortality and accountability. The small adornments atop these large groups are easily damaged, and restorers sometimes grind down the remains. The two figures at either end, one holding a sword and the other a Bible, are tyler masons. Their task is to ensure that only those permitted to attend Masonic meetings are admitted. The tyler masons also occur as individual figures (Vol. 1, figs. 25.51–52) and on rare watch stands (Vol. 3, fig. 126.147, Vol. 4, figs. 199.44–45).

The figures portraying a cherub and titled *PREPARE TO MEET THY GOD* represent the Archangel Gabriel, the biblical messenger (fig. 110.3–4). Similar figures without this titling are shown among the cherubs in volume 4, chapter 197.

Figure 110.1. *PREPARE TO MEET THY GOD*. Attributed to "Sherratt." H: 12.6", L: 10.2". The base is specific to "Sherratt." Price C. *Collection of Arnold and Barbara Berlin.*

Figure 110.2. *PREPARE TO MEET THY GOD*. Attributed to "Sherratt." H: ~10". Table bases of this form are characteristic of "Sherratt." Price C.

Figure 110.3. *PREPARE TO MEET THY GOD*. Attributed to "Sherratt." H: ~8.6". The floral sprigs applied to the mound support the attribution. Price B.

Figure 110.4. *PREPAER TO MEET THY GOD*. H: ~8". Price B. *John Howard; www.antiquepottery.co.uk.*

Notes

34. Ophelia
1. Christie's South Kensington, June 11, 1992, lot 93.

49. Maria Malibran
1. P. D. Gordon Pugh, *Staffordshire Portrait Figures of the Victorian Age*. (Woodbridge, Suffolk: Antique Collectors' Club, 1987), 450.

51. Paul Pry
1. Christie's South Kensington, July 24, 1997, 7679, lot 43.

55. Billy Waters and Douglas
1. For example, Theatre Royal Edinburgh, December 26, 1822.

58. Dick Turpin
1. Christie's South Kensington, October 28, 1993, lot 117.

60. Unidentified Theatrical Figures
1. Bonhams Knightsbridge, December 15, 1993, lot 39.

67. Duke of Clarence or Duke of York
1. Peter Bradshaw, *18ᵗʰ Century English Porcelain Figures*. (Woodbridge, Suffolk: Antique Collectors' Club, 1981), 405, 406, 460.
2. Ibid, 394–5.

68. Oliver Cromwell
1. Jonathan Horne, *A Collection of Early English Pottery, Parts I to X 1981–1990*. (London: Jonathan Horne, 1981–1990), *Part IV, #103*.

72. John Milton
1. Julia Poole, *Plagiarism Personified*. (Cambridge: Fitzwilliam Museum, 1986), 26–27.
2. Reginald Haggar, *Staffordshire Chimney Ornaments*. (London: Phoenix House, 1955), plate 13.

74. William Shakespeare
1. Frank Falkner, *The Wood Family of Burslem*. (London: Chapman & Hall, 1912), 92.

81. Boxing
1. Myrna Schkolne, *People, Passions, Pastimes, and Pleasures: Staffordshire Figures 1810–1835*. (Winston-Salem, NC: Hot Lane Press, 2006), 152–159.

89. Crucifixion
1. John Hall, *Staffordshire Portrait Figures*. (New York: World Pub., 1972), 22–23, for an example described as "John Walton (impressed)." The mark is not shown, and this description is thought to be erroneous. Note that the Walton mark never includes "John."

103. Saints Matthew, Mark, Luke, and John
1. Christie's South Kensington, May 19, 2005, lot 1020.

104. Saint Paul
1. Christie's South Kensington, May 19, 2005, lot 1020.

108. The Tithe Pig
1. R. K. Price, *Astbury, Whieldon, and Ralph Wood Figures, and Toby Jugs*. (London: John Lane, 1992), plate LXVV.

109. Religious Officials and Observers
1. An example marked in this way was donated to Australia's Powerhouse Museum in 1927, evidencing that the group was produced before that date.

Bibliography

Bradshaw, Peter. *18th Century English Porcelain Figures.* Woodbridge, Suffolk: Antique Collectors' Club, 1981.

_____. *Derby Porcelain Figures 1750–1848.* London: Faber & Faber, 1990.

Cox, Alwyn and Angela Cox. *Rockingham 1745–1842.* Woodbridge, Suffolk: Antique Collectors' Club, 2001.

Dudson, Audrey M. and Alison Morgan. *Dudson Staffordshire Figures.* Stoke-on-Trent: Dudson Publications, 2006.

Earle, Cyril. *The Earle Collection of Early Staffordshire Pottery.* London: Brown, 1915.

Edwards, Diana. *Neale Pottery and Porcelain, its Predecessors and Successors 1763–1829.* London: Barrie & Jenkins, 1987.

Edwards, Diana and Rodney Hampson. *English Dry-Bodied Stoneware: Wedgwood and Contemporary Manufacturers 1774–1830.* Woodbridge, Suffolk: Antique Collectors' Club, 1998.

Falkner, Frank. *The Wood Family of Burslem.* London: Chapman & Hall, 1912.

Godden, Geoffrey A. *Encyclopaedia of British Pottery and Porcelain Marks.* London: Barrie & Jenkins, 1991.

Goodacre, J.M. *A Catalogue of the Goodacre Collection of Early Staffordshire Pottery Figures.* N.p.: Goodacre, 2007.

Grigsby, Leslie. *English Pottery 1650–1800: The Henry K. Weldon Collection.* London: Sotheby's Publications, 1990.

Haggar, Reginald. *Staffordshire Chimney Ornaments.* London: Phoenix House, 1955.

Halfpenny, Pat. *English Earthenware Figures 1780–1840.* Woodbridge, Suffolk: Antique Collectors' Club, 1991.

Halfpenny, Patricia and Stella Beddoe. *Circus and Sport.* Louisville, Kentucky: J.B. Speed Art Museum, 1990.

Hall, John, *Staffordshire Portrait Figures.* New York: World Pub., 1972.

Hamilton-Foyn, Wynne. "Who Modelled and Made Ralph Wood Figures?" Unpublished research, 2009. Copies held at the Victoria and Albert Museum, British Museum, Potteries Museum, Fitzwilliam Museum, Ashmolean Museum, and Wedgwood Museum.

Hampson, Rodney. *Pottery References in the Staffordshire Advertiser, 1795–1865.* Hanley: Northern Ceramic Society, 2000.

Hayden, Arthur. *Chats on English Earthenware.* London: Unwin, 1909.

Henrywood, R. K. *Staffordshire Potters 1781–1900.* Woodbridge: Antique Collectors' Club, 2002.

Hodkinson, H. M. and Judith Hodkinson. *Sherratt? A Natural Family of Staffordshire Figures.* London: Chisquare, 1991.

Horne, Jonathan. *A Collection of Early English Pottery, Parts I to X 1981–1990.* London: Jonathan Horne, 1981–1990.

_____. *A Collection of Early English Pottery, Parts XI to XX 1991–2000.* London: Jonathan Horne, 1991–2000.

Hughes, J. F. *Recollections of Old Liverpool by a Nonagerian.* Liverpool, 1836.

Jewitt, Llewellynn. *The Wedgwoods: being a life of Josiah Wedgwood; with notices of his works and their productions, memoirs of the Wedgewood and other families, and a history of the early potteries of Staffordshire.* London, Virtue., 1865.

Jewitt, Llewellynn. *The Ceramic Art of Great Britain.* N.p: Virtue, 1878.

Kiddell, A. J. B. "William Absolon of Yarmouth," *English Ceramic Circle Transactions,* 5:1 (1960), 53–64.

John, W. D., and Warren Baker. *Old English Lustre Ware.* New York: Walker, 1966.

Lewis, Griselda. *A Collector's History of English Pottery.* Woodbridge, Suffolk: Antique Collectors' Club, 1985.

Lewis, John, and Griselda Lewis. *Pratt Ware: English and Scottish Relief Decorated and Underglaze Coloured Earthenware.* Woodbridge, Suffolk: Antique Collectors' Club, 2006.

Locket, T. A. and P. A. Halfpenny, eds. *Creamware and Pearlware Re-Examined.* Stoke-on-Trent, City Museum and Art Gallery, 1989.

Manheim, Emily. *Selections from the Hope McCormick Collection of Staffordshire Pottery.* Chicago, 1980.

McVeigh, Patrick. *Scottish East Coast Potteries.* Edinburgh: Donald, 1979.

Oliver, Anthony. *Staffordshire Pottery: the Tribal Art of England.* London: Heinemann, 1981.

Poole, Julia. *Plagiarism Personified.* Cambridge: Fitzwilliam Museum, 1986.

Price, R. K. *Astbury, Whieldon, and Ralph Wood Figures, and Toby Jugs.* London: John Lane, 1992.

Pugh, P. D. Gordon, *Staffordshire Portrait Figures of the Victorian Age.* Woodbridge, Suffolk: Antique Collectors' Club, 1987.

Rackham, Bernard. *Catalogue of the Glaisher Collection of Pottery & Porcelain in the Fitzwilliam Museum, Cambridge.* Woodbridge, Suffolk: Antique Collectors' Club, 1987.

Read, Herbert. *Staffordshire Pottery Figures.* London: Duckworth, 1929.

Roden, Peter. *Copyhold Potworks and Housing in the Staffordshire Potteries, 1700–1832.* Cumbria: Wood Broughton Publications, 2008.

Schkolne, Myrna. "A Pearlware Puzzle: Walton Figures and Their Look-Alikes," *American Ceramic Circle Journal,* XVI (2011), 56–77.

_____. *People, Passions, Pastimes, and Pleasures: Staffordshire Figures 1810–1835.* Winston-Salem, NC: Hot Lane Press, 2006.

Stanley, Louis T. *Collecting Staffordshire Pottery.* New York: Doubleday, 1963.

Staffordshire Education Dept. *A Directory of the Staffordshire Potteries.* Stafford: Staffordshire County Council, 1982.

Ward, John. *The Borough of Stoke-upon-Trent.* London: Lewis, 1843.

Walton, Peter. *Creamware and Other English Pottery at Temple Newsam House, Leeds.* Bradford, UK, Manningham, 1976.

Williams, Peter, and Pat Halfpenny. *A Passion for Pottery.* New York: Sotheby's, 2000.

Index

Italics denote titled figures
The number in **bold font** preceding page numbers indicates
the relevant Volume number

270

272